THE LETTERED CITY

A Book in the Series

Latin America in Translation/En Traducción/Em Tradução

Sponsored by the Duke–University of North Carolina

Joint Program in Latin American Studies

Post-Contemporary Interventions

Series Editors: Stanley Fish and Fredric Jameson

Angel Rama

The Lettered City

Edited and Translated by John Charles Chasteen

Duke University Press Durham and London 1996

#34473694

Translation of the books in the series Latin America in Translation/En

Traducción/Em Tradução, a collaboration between the Duke–University of North

Carolina Joint Program in Latin American Studies and the university presses of

Duke and the University of North Carolina, is supported by a grant from

the Andrew W. Mellon Foundation.

CONTENTS

John Charles Chasteen

INTRODUCTION

 Writing, urbanism, and the state have had a special relationship in Latin America. To impose order on vast empires, the Iberian monarchs created precocious urban networks, carefully planned with pen and paper, their geometrical layout standardized by detailed written instructions. New cities housed both the institutions of state power and the writers who dealt in edicts, memoranda, reports, and all the official correspondence that held the empire together. So began close, enduring links of large importance in Latin American life and literature, a nexus of lettered culture, state power, and urban location that Angel Rama calls *la ciudad letrada,* the lettered city.[1]

The brokers of this relationship were a group of men called *letrados* — a "lettered" elite closely associated with the institutions of state and invariably urban in orientation. Written documents articulated the Spanish and Portuguese empires, ideologically and organically, and their ability to write the official language of empire gave the letrados privileged access to power. Imagine them: bearded and

1. Rama chose the phrase *la ciudad letrada,* the lettered city, for his key interpretive construct instead of the alternative *la ciudad de las letras,* the city of letters. "The city of letters" suggests a less exclusive metropolis, inhabited by signs and all those who can manipulate them. Significantly, Rama's choice of words emphasizes the distinction between the "lettered" and the merely "literate." Although generally preferring "the lettered city" (e.g., in the title of the book), I have allowed for considerable stylistic variation and treated the two phrases as equivalent. Another translation worth noting is John Beverley's "the republic of letters," which effectively conveys the corporate spirit of the letrados but loses the crucial reference to urbanism: John Beverley, *Against Literature* (Minneapolis: University of Minnesota Press, 1993).

My thanks to Lucia Binotti for help with the French and Italian passages.

grave, the letrados of the colonial period are privy to the theocratic mysteries of empire. They can prove surprising things by quoting irrefutable authorities in Latin or cut a quill to correspond with the ministers of the king. The frock-coated lawyers of the nineteenth century, who quote English authorities more avidly than Latin ones during their parliamentary perorations, are the colonial letrados' direct successors as inhabitants of the lettered city (whether or not they descended from the same families), so are the 1920s city slickers whose cars throw whole villages into an uproar as they jolt across a Latin American countryside less familiar to them than the streets of Paris.

Today, bundle after bundle of yellowed, frayed-edged archival documents lie in dusty, silent stacks throughout what was the Spanish or the Portuguese empire in America. If tropical humidity and worms have been kept out, sturdy paper has often withstood the test of time fairly well — much better than electronic records will ever do. Careful columns of dark-inked script are organized according to standardized protocols of spacing, so that the main column often stands quite off center, run up against the right edge of the page with a wide margin on the left for notations as the document wends its way through bureaucratic channels. These are internal documents, so to speak, of the city of letters. Their capital letters with grand flourishes bespeak authority, and the undersigned elaborate signatures serve as guarantees of documentary authenticity. Here are the personnel records of faithful (and unfaithful) bureaucrats and military men, periodic reports produced by a variety of official bodies and functionaries, and petitions for pensions and for privileges of a thousand kinds — to be considered white, to purchase a title of nobility, to avoid capital punishment. Then, of course, there are the records of notaries and of the many judges who handled so many functions of governance: criminal trials, divisions of inheritance, and interminable lawsuits.

As Rama points out, writing was an everyday practice in the lettered city. Administrative and judicial documents are the principal surviving embodiment of that practice. Other vestiges are the parish registers of churches, where local curates maintained the only official records of births, marriages, and deaths. There were also private letters traveling back and forth across the Atlantic by the hundreds and thousands from the very beginning of colonization, but only a tiny portion of them survive. Despite poetic exercises aplenty and even some long treatises of various (mostly theological) kinds, writing tended to circulate in extremely narrow, usually official, channels. Those who wrote had special access to the power of the colonial state but also depended on the state for a livelihood.

Rama's discussion of the lettered city of the colonial period brings post-colonial continuities and contrasts into clear focus. Literacy and education expanded gradually but remained the possessions of a privileged few until the end of the nineteenth century. Still, national independence brought a new bustle to the lettered city. The pursuit and exercise of elective office had suddenly become a booming enterprise, and it was open only to the lettered. The letrados would now give innumerably more speeches (usually of a ponderously rhetorical kind, carefully written out beforehand, appealing to history and to the most respected "classical and modern authors" to advance their arguments) and they now would write laws instead of merely applying and interpreting them as before. The prestige of their language, nevertheless, came from its connection to a lettered culture centered in Europe, just as had been true in the colonial period. Meanwhile, the letrados had also begun to exercise a new sort of influence as spokesmen of this or that group in the new public sphere of debate on issues of the *res publica*. The result was a significant expansion of all sorts of publishing, most especially that of the periodical press.

Rama shows how newspapers played an essential role in the evolution of the lettered city, particularly in the slow process whereby some letrados eventually made themselves economically independent of the state. Ephemeral publications of various kinds multiplied startlingly in the wake of independence — not everywhere, of course, but especially in capital cities where letrados congregated. Many sheets were short-lived productions of a single person who aimed to promote a political cause rather than to provide news. Even the more substantial newspapers did little reporting of local events in the early nineteenth century, devoting vastly more space and emphasis to politics, commerce, and affairs of state, with a novel published by installment at the bottom of the page. During the second half of the nineteenth century, newspapers multiplied rapidly outside the capital cities, so that by the end of the century even quite small towns might have a couple of biweeklies, single sheets folded to make four pages, mostly ads on pages three and four. Today they slouch against each other in bindings weakened by age, and the brittle newsprint of the late nineteenth century — ironically much more fragile than the archival documents of the sixteenth or seventeenth century — has not lasted well. The huge format adopted by many of the period's major dailies makes them especially fragile. The pages of many collections cannot be turned without shattering, and many others have already crumbled into dust.

What about books? What, in a word, about *literature*? The same letrados who drew up legal documents, delivered patriotic harangues, and aired their partisan opinions day after day in the newspaper also wrote the essays, fiction, and verse that compose the various national literary canons of Latin America. The titles of many of the first books published in the region are indicative of the letrados' activities in other venues. The *Relation of the case brought against Col. don Fabio José Maines for a supposed insult inferred by the press against the honor of individuals who were officers of the Volunteers for Liberty Battalion* (1840), for example, seems the lawyerly sort of document that might formerly have been sent to the king but was now addressed to the court of public opinion. And, no matter how practical minded his other writings, each young letrado must publish his own slender, poignant volume of poetry (though it be at his own expense) as a testimony to his coming of age. It was normal for the same man — a sometime elected representative and lifetime inhabitant of the lettered city — to author a wide array of books: stirring portraits of founding heroes and vitriolic condemnations of tyrants; pragmatic treatises on the advisability of planting alfalfa, dredging harbors, requiring vaccinations for smallpox, or limiting the number of professional degrees granted each year; fictional works (novels running the gamut from romanticism to naturalism, collections of short stories first published in the newspaper); and theatrical literature, including plays that caused a sensation, plays that closed on the third night, and plays that were never performed at all. Like the periodical press, the volume of book production rose markedly, if not hugely, in the immediate aftermath of independence, then expanded more quickly (along with literacy rates) in the late nineteenth and early twentieth centuries.

It is precisely the period from 1880 to 1920 that Rama examines in greatest detail. During these years, the lettered city reached out into the countryside to describe landscapes, document folkways, and collect oral traditions — all useful in the elaboration of official national cultures and literatures. The lettered city thus incorporated and appropriated popular culture more than ever before. At the same time, the advance of public education facilitated the inculcation of social norms conceived by, and particularly benefiting, the lettered elite. Yet wider literacy created a market for periodicals and books that enabled some writers — formerly held in thrall by wealthy patrons or state sinecures — to shake off their economic dependence on the state and escape its tutelage. For the first time, writers could leave the lettered city, so to speak, and write from outside it. Now they could even publish condemnations of the letrados' monopoly on the written word and pursue agendas that led toward more inclusive, more democratic definitions of national community. Therefore, Rama abandons the bold, simple lines with which he sketched the creation of the lettered city and its success in weathering the transition from a colonial to a post-colonial order to paint, in the closing chapters, a fully textured portrait of the complex — sometimes contradictory — cultural reverberations of "modernization" and nationalism.

The paradigmatic clarity of the interpretation naturally wanes as Rama gives more attention to particular currents and countercurrents. The stark initial view of writing as an instrument of state power, for example, is partly offset by an optimistic assessment of the liberating potential of inclusive nationalism and public education.

Indeed, the elitist citadel of letters finally succumbs to an insurgency conducted, at least partially, in writing. Just how this occurs is not entirely explained, however.

Rama makes most vigorous use of the concept of the lettered city at the outset, when literacy was virtually synonymous with elevated social status. During the colonial period the letrados were a handful of literate, white, upper-class males who stood almost inevitably within reach of the social levers of power. Gradually, however, the circle of literacy widened beyond a handful of European administrators, and the social boundaries of the lettered city become less precise. By the nineteenth century, there were some — not a large portion of the population, by any means, but some — non-elite men and women who had learned to read and write and yet lacked access to the power and privileges associated with the lettered city. Conversely, some who did gain power and influence around the turn of the twentieth century were engineers, physicians, or agronomists whose training emphasized applied science rather than rhetoric, literature, history, or law. It becomes rather difficult, by the end, to know who should be included in the lettered city. This is, after all, a posthumous book, and Rama's untimely death may be responsible for the interpretation's gradual loosening and relative lack of closure.

Rama's powerful interpretive construct nevertheless integrates the book, and it potentially integrates much else, as well, by obliging us to contemplate long-term continuities and allowing us to perceive unexpected relationships among, for example, a notarized deed, a regionalist short story, and the nomenclature of city streets. It shows how literature is embedded in history, provides a basic map of the historical sociology of writing, and abounds in particular insights about everything from colonial graffiti to the novels of the Mexican Revolution. Any student of Latin American literature or cultural studies must explore the implications of the lettered city, as should anyone who wonders how Iberian empires were created and maintained, anyone mystified by the dynamics of post-independence politics, or anyone fascinated by the complex historical relationship between European and Latin American culture. In short, *The Lettered*

City offers a conceptual reader's guide for virtually everything written in Latin America between 1500 and 1920.

The Lettered City should be a required text particularly for those exploring the phenomenon of cultural hegemony. As an aspect of rule, cultural hegemony implies an indirectness that differentiates it from the total dominance of superior coercive force. Often, hegemony involves a vigorous give-and-take between those who exercise power and those who resist it, but the outcome is always some measure of consent. Rule by the privileged few, characteristic of most of Latin America for half a millennium, seldom succeeds for long without widespread consent. Recently, and for readily understandable reasons, interpreters of Latin America have preferred to dwell on the story of popular resistance within this larger picture. Resistance studies offer the stirring and salutary message that the people of Latin America have often tenaciously defied exploitative rule. Popular resistance is inspiring, but it is not the whole story. The full annals of cultural hegemony make more sobering but no less vital reading and oblige us to contemplate the hegemonic power that operates at the level of people's basic assumptions. The most devastating effects of cultural hegemony occur when hierarchies of race and class, for example, are made to appear aspects of the natural order rather than results of a project of domination. The prestige of "lettered" culture sprang precisely from such a hegemonic effect. Those outside the spell of the letrados' language can easily sneer at their overblown rhetoric, and twentieth-century fiction often satirizes it. On the other hand, whether in Mexico or Brazil or Rama's native Uruguay, rare is the literary depiction of a self-important letrado that does not also indicate the awe generally attached to the language of power.

Therefore, although "Latin America" is too large and diverse to be a useful category for many sorts of analysis, Rama has good reason to use it here. Indeed, his emphasis on the colonial origins of the lettered city make such a wide view natural, since the letrados staffed a coherent colonizing project of continental proportions. The parallel developments highlighted by Rama for the nineteenth and early twentieth centuries also amply justify panoramic vistas, and Rama is properly attentive not only to consistent patterns but also to variations within them. Nevertheless, as is probably inevitable despite his impressive breadth of knowledge, he tends to understand the region principally through the parts of it that he knows best. He takes examples most frequently from the Río de la Plata, and there is also something Rioplatense in his general emphasis on the rural/urban dichotomy, in the stress he lays on expanding literacy at the beginning of the twentieth century, and in the relatively minor roles played in his interpretation by indigenous populations. In addition, Rama's discussion of imperial urban utopias hardly applies to Portuguese America at all. Brazilian settlements showed a greater tendency to spring up informally, where trade roots intersected or natural harbors beckoned, and the checkerboard street plan typical of Spanish American cities did not govern the layout of colonial Brazilian cities. The social exclusivity of the lettered city, on the other hand, was even more marked in Brazil than in much of Spanish America, making Rama's interpretation quite relevant to understanding Brazilian literature and history.

All generalizations have exceptions, but without generalizing one simply cannot get very far in making sense of large, complex aspects of collective experience. Overall, Rama's interpretation gains much from its audacious assertions and its bold attempt to span centuries and embrace so much of the hemisphere. Had he been more timid, the lettered city might have long remained a dimly perceived curiosity, tentatively remarked in reference to isolated phenomena in one country or another, and not at all what Rama has given us: a basic key to understanding the literature and history of an entire world region.

THE LETTERED CITY

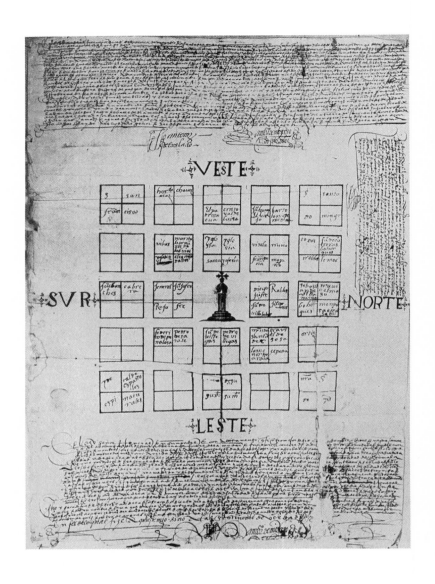

Mendoza

(Ministerio de Educación y Cultura. Archivo General de Indias.)

I

THE ORDERED CITY

 From the remodeling of Tenochtitlán after its destruction by Hernán Cortés in 1521, to the 1960 inauguration of that most fabulous dream city of the Americas, Lúcio Costa's and Oscar Niemeyer's Brasília, Latin American cities have ever been creations of the human mind. The ideal of the city as the embodiment of social order corresponded to a moment in the development of Western civilization as a whole, but only the lands of the new continent afforded a propitious place for the dream of the "ordered city" to become a reality.

Over the course of the sixteenth century, the Spanish conquerors became aware of having left behind the distribution of space and the way of life characteristic of the medieval Iberian cities — "organic," rather than "ordered" — where they had been born and raised. Gradually and with difficulty, they adapted themselves to a frankly rationalizing vision of an urban future, one that ordained a planned and repetitive urban landscape and also required that its inhabitants be organized to meet increasingly stringent requirements of colonization, administration, commerce, defense, and religion.

Upon crossing the Atlantic ocean, they had passed from an old continent to a "new" one and had also entered a different era, animated by an expansive and ecumenical sort of capitalism still charged with a medieval sense of mission. The avenues toward this new era of Western culture had been opened by the Renaissance spirit of its sixteenth-century designers but would be perfected only later by the absolute monarchies. The absolutist European nation states of the seventeenth and eighteenth centuries enjoyed the full support of religious institutions and focused their power at the royal court, seeking to impose from there a hierarchical discipline on the rest of society. The points of juncture between the ideal ordering impulse and the existing social reality produced an enduring urban model: the Baroque city.[1]

This ordering impulse could do relatively little to transform the old cities of Europe, where the stubbornly material sediments of the past encumbered the flight of a designer's fancy, but it found a unique opportunity in the virgin territory of an enormous continent. There, native urbanistic values were blindly erased by the Iberian conquerors to create a supposedly "blank slate," though the outright denial of impressive indigenous cultures would not, of course, prevent them from surviving quietly to infiltrate the conquering culture later.[2] Having cleared the ground, the city builders erected an edifice that, even when imagined as a mere transposition of European antecedents, in fact represented the urban dream of a new age. The cities of Spanish America were the first material realization of that dream, giving them a central role in the advent of world capitalism.[3]

Although the conquerors appended the adjective *new* to familiar regional names (New Spain, New Galicia, New Granada) in designating portions of their recently acquired territory, and though they vacillated initially under the lingering influence of Iberian cities like those from which they had originally set out, they did not reproduce those cities in America.[4] Gradually, through trial and error, they filtered the legacy of the past through the clarifying, rationalizing, and systematizing experience of colonization, in the "stripping down process" described by George M. Foster.[5] Thus, the patterns of urbanization that they had known firsthand at home were superseded in America by ideal models implemented with routine uniformity in accordance with the vastness and systematic planning of the imperial enterprise.

The ideas of *The Republic,* revived by Renaissance humanism, arrived in America through the same Neoplatonist cultural channels that guided the advance of Iberian capitalism. And with Neoplatonic idealism came the influence of the quasi-mythical Hippodamus, Greek father of the ideal city—especially his "confidence that the processes of reason could impose measure and order on every human activity."[6] The imposition of these ideas in the sixteenth and seventeenth centuries corresponds to that crucial moment in Western culture when, as Michel Foucault has sagaciously perceived, words began to separate from things, and people's understanding of epistemology changed from one of triadic conjuncture to the binary relationship expressed in the *Logique* of Port Royal, published in 1662, theorizing the independence of the "order of signs."[7] The cities of Spanish America, the societies that were to inhabit them, and the "lettered" interpreters of them developed together in a time when signs became no longer "direct representations of the world, linked to it by secret, solid ties of likeness or affinity with what they represent," and began instead "to signify from within a body of knowledge" and "to take from it their probability or certainty."[8]

From that flow of knowledge sprang forth the ideal cities of the Iberian empires' American vastness. Their ordering principle revealed itself as a hierarchical society transposed by analogy into a hierarchical design of urban space. It was not the real society that was transposed, of course, but its organized form, and not into the fabric of the living city, but merely into its ideal layout, so that in the geometrical distribution we can read the social morphology of the planners. This conversion was made possible by the advancing project of rationalization. The untrammeled rationalizing urge demanded similar flexibility in the order of signs. Rationalization also required a concentration of power to implement the directives of the rationalizers. That power was already visibly temporal and human, although it cloaked and legitimated itself ideologically in celestial absolutes, as power will do. Such legitimation had long been provided by religion, but when the religious masks of power were shattered, stately secular ideologies soon substituted them. In a like manner, efforts to legitimate existing power relations have always been the great source of new ideologies.

The lexical key to the entire imperial system was the Janus-faced word *order,* symptomatically ambiguous in grammatical gender (*el orden* or *la orden*), a concept pursued equally by the church, the army, and the administrative bureaucracy of the Iberian empires. According to the received definitions of the day, order meant: "putting things in their places; concert and harmonious disposition among things; the rule or mode to be observed in producing things." Pursuit of order lay at the heart of the systems of classification (like natural history, architecture, and geometry) that then loomed so large in the corpus of knowledge. The word *order* recurs obsessively in the instructions imparted in 1513 by the king, or rather by his council of advisers, to Pedrarias Dávila, leader of a Spanish expedition that pushed beyond the conquistadors' original foothold in the Caribbean once accommodation to the New World environment had readied them for further violent expansion and colonization. It is worthy of emphasis, though hardly surprising, that the instructions framed the entire enterprise in terms of Spanish colonial interests, establishing from the very first a coastal orientation and a string of port cities that would, centuries later, undermine attempts at national integration in not a few independent states. Point number seven of the instructions fixed the following guidelines for cities to be founded on the new continent:

Having ascertained what things are necessary for the settlements and having chosen the site most advantageous and abundantly provided with all things necessary to those who will settle therein, distribute town lots for the construction of houses, in *orderly* fashion, according to the quality of the recipients, so that, once constructed, the town will appear well-*ordered* as regards the space designated for the central plaza, the location of the church, and the placement of the streets; because where such *orders* are given from the outset, *orderly* results will follow without undue cost and effort, and in other places *order* will never be achieved.[9]

Thus, beyond the immediate needs of urban planning, rationalized cities reflected a vision of the future. The transference of an idealized social order into the physical reality of the newly founded cities required the previous cultural elaboration of rationalizing symbolic languages. The royal directives sought quite explicitly to program eventual social development in accord with the vision of the rationalizers, and they were aided in this endeavor by the period's most abstract symbolic language: mathematics. The methods of analytical geometry had recently been extended to all areas of human endeavor by Descartes, who regarded them as the only valid — unerring and uncontaminated — tools of reason.

When applied to urban planning in Spanish America, the result was the ubiquitous checkerboard grid that has endured practically until the present day. Other geometric designs might have affected the same transference of social ideal into urban reality. Circular plans constituted a frequent option in Renaissance thinking, derived from the teaching of Vitruvio and visible in the works of León Batista Alberti, Jacopo Barozzi Vignola, Antonio Arvelino Filareta, and Andrea Pallacio, among others.[10] The circular layout responded to the same regulating principles as the checkerboard: unity, planning, and rigorous order reflecting a social hierarchy. Circular plans perhaps conveyed even more precisely than square ones the social hierarchy desired by the planners, with governing authority located at the center and the living spaces assigned to respective social strata radiating from the center in concentric circles. Both designs were simply variations of the same conception, in which the application of reason imposed a specific order on social reality through the engineer's "taut line and rule," as the royal instructions to the advancing conquerors frequently specified verbatim.

As Michel Foucault observed, "what made the classical episteme possible as a whole, of course, was its relationship to a knowledge of order."[11] In the case of cities, that indispensable knowledge resulted in the principle of urban planning. The Enlightenment, that epoch of faith in rational operations, further strengthened and institutionalized the planning impulse, and concern over the outcomes of urban planning elicited spirited commentary on its designs, its procedures, and above all, its guiding philosophies.[12]

More important than the much-discussed grid design are the general principles behind it, directing a whole series of transmitted directives (from Spain to America, from the governing head to the physical body of the city) so that the distribution of urban space would reproduce and confirm the desired social order. But even more important is the principle postulated in the quoted directives of the king: before anything may be built, the city must be *imagined* in order to avoid circumstances that might interfere with its ordained norms. The notion that statutory order must be constituted at the outset to prevent future disorder alludes to the peculiar virtue of signs: to remain unalterable despite the passage of time and, at least hypothetically, to constrain changing reality in a changeless rational framework. Operating on these principles, the Iberian empires established rigid procedures for founding new cites and then extended them methodically across vast stretches of time and space.

Before their appearance as material entities, cities had to be constructed as symbolic representations. Therefore, the permanence of the whole depended on the immutability of the signs themselves — on the words that transmitted the will to build the city in accordance with the stipulated norms — and also on the diagrams that translated the will into graphic terms. Without drawn plans the mental image created by the written directives was more likely to suffer permutations owing to local conditions or to inexpert execution. *Thinking the city* was the function of these symbolic systems, and their growing autonomy suited them increasingly to the manipulations of absolute authority.

The conquerors still asserted territorial claims through rituals impregnated with magic, but now they required a writer of some sort (a scribe, a notary, a chronicler) to cast their foundational acts in the form of imperishable signs. The resulting scripture had the high function reserved to notarial documents, which according to the Spanish formula, give witness or "faith" to the acts they record. The prestige that could only derive from the written word thus began its portentous imperial career on the American continent.

In Latin America, the written word became the only binding one — in contradistinction to the spoken word, which belonged to the realm of things precarious and uncertain. It even seemed plausible that (contrary to Saussure) spoken language derived from written language rather than vice versa. Writing boasted a permanence, a kind of autonomy from the material world, that imitated eternity and appeared free from the vicissitudes and metamorphoses of history.

Above all, writing consolidated the political order by giving it rigorously elaborated cultural expression. Over the framework provided by linguistic discourse, the planners stretched the canvas of graphic design. Not subject to the semantic multiplicity of words, this second layer of signs surpassed the virtue of the first as an instrument of urban planning. Drawn diagrams fused the thing represented (the city) with the representation (the drawing) in haughty independence from mundane realities, as period descriptions reveal. Of the 1535 founding of Lima by Pizarro (so criticized among thinkers of a later independent Peru), we learn that the city "was laid out and established according to the plan, and the drawing of it, which had been done on paper."

Drawn plans have always been the best examples of operative cultural models. Behind their ostensible function as neutral registers of reality lies an ideological framework that validates and organizes that reality, authorizing all sorts of intellectual extrapolations on the model. Clifford Geertz makes recourse to this example to define ideology as a cultural system,[13] and it may be traced back to the seventeenth-century *Logique* of Port Royal, which sought to establish a difference between "the ideas pertaining to things and those pertaining to signs," thereby codifying the modern notion. The *Logique* also appealed to the model represented by maps and drawn plans, in which reality is somehow absorbed by the signs that stand for it:

When one considers an object in and of itself, within its own being, without transferring the view of the spirit to that which it could represent, the idea one has is the idea of a thing, like the idea of the earth or the sun. But when one looks at a certain object as merely referring to another, one has the idea of a sign, and so it may be called. Ordinarily, this is the way one regards maps or tableaux. Thus, a sign contains two ideas — one, of the thing represented, and the other, of the thing doing the representing — and it is in the nature of signs that the first idea is evoked by the second.[14]

In order to sustain their argument, the *Logique*'s authors Arnauld and Nicole must first suppose that the object will be perceived as a sign, a basic thought operation that does not depend on the diagrams themselves. Furthermore, the authors do not admit the degree to which the diagrams — along with their function of representing something else — acquire a certain autonomy of their own. Among the principles they derive from the discussion, Arnauld and Nicole conclude that signs possess a permanence remote from the limited lives of things. As long as a sign exists its immutability is guaranteed, even though the object represented may have been destroyed long since — hence the unalterability of the universe of signs, not subject to physical decay but only to the operations of hermeneutics. "One could conclude that the nature of signs consists in stimulating, within the mind, the image of the thing represented by the application of the thing doing the representing. As long as the effect continues, that is to say, as long as the double idea is evoked, the sign endures, even though the thing represented may itself have been destroyed."[15] From here, it is easy to invert the process: instead of representing things already existing, signs can be made to represent things as yet only imagined — the ardently desired objects of an age that displayed a special fondness for utopian dreams. Thus, the manipulation of signs opened the way to a futurism characteristic of the modern era, an attitude that has attained an almost delirious apotheosis in our own day. The dreams of a future order served to perpetuate the reigning political power and its attendant social, economic, and cultural structures. In addition, any discourse raised in opposition to the reigning power was required, henceforth, to establish credibility by presenting an alternative dream of the future.

Accordingly, from the time of their foundation the imperial cities of Latin America had to lead double lives: on one hand, a material life inescapably subject to the flux of construction and destruction, the contrary impulses of restoration and renovation, and the circumstantial intervention of human agency; on the other hand, a symbolic life, subject only to the rules governing the order of signs, which enjoy a stability impervious to the accidents of the physical world. Before becoming a material reality of houses, streets, and plazas, which could be constructed only gradually over decades or centuries, Latin American cities sprang forth in signs and plans, already complete, in the documents that laid their statutory foundations and in the charts and plans that established their ideal designs. These visions rarely escaped the pitfall of rationalized futures, the fatal principle of mechanical regularity that Thomas More exemplified and glorified in his own *Utopia* of 1516: "He who knows one of the cities will know them all, so exactly alike are they, except where the nature of the ground prevents."

The dreams of architects (Alberti, Filarete, and Vitruvio) and designers of utopias (More, Campanella) came to little in material terms, but they fortified the order of signs, extending the rhetorical capacity of this instrument of absolutism to impose hierarchical order on sprawling empires. Born of circumstances specific to the age, the influence of these urbanistic designs far outlasted it. Such is the nature of the order signs that it privileges potentiality over reality, creating frameworks that, if not eternal, have lasted at least until the late twentieth century. Even more rooted has been the capacity of the order of signs, in moments when its old formulas appear exhausted, to rearticulate itself, preserving and even strengthening its central principle of hierarchy amid new historical circumstances.

This capacity of the order of signs to configure the future was complemented symmetrically by an ability to erase the past. The fifteenth and sixteenth centuries, far from effecting a renaissance of classicism, transported it to the universe of pure form, and thus established the splendorous first cultural model of modernity, harbinger of the grander transubstantiation of the past that would be propagated by eighteenth- and nineteenth-century historicism. Renaissance palingenesis facilitated European seaborne expansion much as, a few hundred years later, Enlightenment palingenesis laid the foundation of European world domination. In their rewritings of the past, according to Peter Gay's sympathetic description, historians of the period contributed to a larger systematic effort "to secure rational control of the world, reliable knowledge of the past, freedom from the pervasive domination of myth."[16]

Modern historians, economists, and philosophers increasingly recognize the tremendous impact that the "discovery" and colonization of America had on the development of Europe—not merely in socioeconomic but also in cultural terms. One could say that the American continent became the experimental field for the formulation of a new Baroque culture. The first methodical application of Baroque ideas was carried out by absolute monarchies in their New World empires, applying rigid principles—abstraction, rationalization, and systematization—and opposing all local expressions of particularity, imagination, or invention. The overbearing power of the order of signs became most intense in those regions that much later received the name Latin America. Gathered together and cloaked by the absolute concept called "Spirit," the signs allowed their masters to disregard the objective constraints of practicality and assume a superior, self-legitimating position, where unfettered imagination could require reality to conform to abstract whimsy. This notion did not stem merely from the need to build cities, of course, although cities were its privileged settings, the artificial enclaves in which the autonomous system of symbolic knowledge could function most efficaciously. The planned urbanism of America was simply the most notable concrete application of Baroque cultural patterns that achieved their apogee under the absolutist monarchy of Spain and generally permeated the social life of its peninsular and American subjects.

The style of the Spanish Conquest contributed to the freestanding character of the resulting urban centers. In the words of Pierre Chaunu, the mainland was "opened, explored, and roughly seized during the three initial decades of the sixteenth century at an insane rhythm, never equaled."[17] Quite contrary to the pattern of an incrementally advancing frontier of settlement (as in the early colonization of Brazil or in the expansion of the United States[18]) the Spanish Conquest was a frenetic gallop across continental immensities—along nearly ten thousand kilometers of mountains, rivers, and tropical forests—leaving in its wake a scattering of cities, isolated and practically out of communication from one another, while the territory between the new urban centers continued to be inhabited almost solely by the dismayed indigenous populations. A mere thirty years elapsed between the founding of Panama City by Pedrarias

Dávila and the founding of the city of Concepción (in the south of Chile) by Pedro Valdivia. In the mechanism of military domination, the urban network functioned to provide, first, bases for successive forays of conquering forces, and then, relay stations for the transmission of subsequent imperial directives. By 1550, colonial governments centered in Mexico and Peru had already begun to implement the orders of their respective viceroys, charged with the duty to "preserve in the New World the charismatic character of royal authority, based on the belief that the king ruled by the grace of God."[19]

The conquest triumphantly imposed its cities on a vast and unknown hinterland, certifying and reiterating the Greek conception that contrasted the civilized inhabitants of the polis to the barbarous denizens of the countryside.[20] The urbanization of Spanish America did not recapitulate the process that had constituted the European norm, however. Instead, that process had been precisely inverted. Rather than stemming from agrarian growth that gradually created an urban market and trade center, rural development here followed the creation of the city, which, though initially tiny, was often situated in a fertile, well-watered valley with a view to encouraging agriculture. "I admit my fascination," declared Fernand Braudel, "with the history of these [Spanish] American towns settled before the countryside or at least simultaneously with it."[21] Having instituted these towns and cities according to preestablished norms, Spanish imperial designs frequently resulted in the forced urbanization of settlers who, in their Iberian homeland, had been rural people, many of them never more to return to agararian occupations. From the outset, then, urban life was the Spanish American ideal, no matter how insignificant the settlement where one lived. All now aspired to be *hidalgos* — minor nobility with the title *don* attached to their names — disdaining manual labor and lording it over their slaves and over the indigenous inhabitants who had been entrusted to them by the crown. These urban dwellers had the responsibility of organizing the agricultural production of the surrounding countryside, and they sought to generate wealth as quickly as possible through merciless exploitation of their coerced labor force. Urbanization and nouveaux riches went together, and smaller centers (especially mining towns), too, had more than their share of conspicuous consumption. Vicere-gal edicts officially restricting the use of carriages, horses, and silken garments failed to check the raging appetite for luxuries that, once set as a cultural model by the opulent conquistadors themselves, con-tinued to be imitated by the whole society, including the poorest among the city dwellers, as colorfully described by seventeenth-century traveler Thomas Gage.[22]

The Baroque cities created by this inopportune expansion did not, of course, function in a total vacuum. Fernand Braudel points out in his notable work outlining the early development of world capitalism that "capitalism and economy marched together and inter-penetrated one another, yet remained distinct."[23] Similarly, these "unreal" cities, more than slightly detached from the surrounding landscape, nevertheless took advantage of indigenous social net-works — their agricultural zones, their market centers, and above all, their labor power. By abruptly inserting their new possessions into a capitalist economy, the Spanish did not completely obliterate the preexisting indigenous market economy, which continued to func-tion in the background for centuries, withering only gradually. In-deed, that economy was to be the source of the Spaniards' most aggressive accumulations of wealth and resources, revealing the ex-tent of the extractive violence introduced into indigenous commu-nities by the conquest.

The priority of urbanism within the colonizing project can be gauged by the durability of the Latin American urban ideal. Three centuries after the conquest, in the early years of the region's inde-pendent nations, Domingo Faustino Sarmiento's *Facundo* (1845) continued to present cities as civilizing nodes in a countryside capa-ble of engendering only barbarism. To Sarmiento, cities were the only receptacles capable of accommodating the culture which he wished to import from its European wellsprings (now those of Paris, rather than Madrid) in order to construct a civilized society in Amer-ica. In order to achieve their civilizing mission, the cities founded by the Spanish and the Portuguese had to dominate and impose certain norms on their savage surroundings. The first of these norms was an education centered on literacy—a true obsession of Sarmiento, who devoted much of his life to seeing it instituted in his native Argentina. It was only half a century later, in the midst of urban Brazil's frontal assault on the culture of the countryside, that Euclides da Cunha began to question the Eurocentric premises that he had previously shared with the Argentine thinker. The result was *Os Sertões* (1902), da Cunha's pessimistic account of the butchery at the millenarian settlement called Canudos in the Brazilian backlands, where military force that relied on imported European technology barely prevailed over the settlement's rustic but determined defenders. The other side of city-led "modernization" had revealed itself nakedly and disagreeably.

Far from being mere trading posts, then, the cities created by the unbridled sixteenth-century conquest aspired to become focal points of ongoing colonization. At first, they functioned — more defensively than offensively—as fortresses, walled precincts where the spirit of the polis could be distilled, protected, ideologically elaborated, and prepared to undertake the superior civilizing responsibilities that it was destined to fulfill. Not infrequently, literary texts transported cities to a "divine" plane. The sixteenth-century Mexican priest Fernán González de Eslava provides an example in his *Coloquios espirituales y sacramentales* when he describes the seven forts linking Mexico City to the Zacatecas silver mines (thus securing the safe transport of mineral wealth to the viceregal capital) in terms that transform them into nothing less than the seven sacraments of the Catholic faith.

Isolated amid vast, alien, and hostile spaces, the cities nevertheless undertook first to "evangelize," and later to "educate" their rural hinterlands. Although the first of these verbs was conjugated through religious energies and the second by a secular and agnostic spirit, both referred to essentially the same enterprise of Eurocentric transculturation. In order to accomplish these ends, Latin American cities became the residences of viceroys, governors, and archbishops, the seats of universities, high courts, and inquisitional tribunals, before becoming home to the presidents and legislatures of independent countries. Such institutions were obligatory instruments for the creation and conservation of *order,* above all after two further etymological derivations of that word — subordinate and insubordinate — gained currency in the eighteenth century, according to the philology of Pere Corominas.

By definition, all order implies a perfectly disciplined hierarchy, so that Latin American cities emerged in stratified categories that, notwithstanding the vicissitudes of the passing centuries, continued rigidly keyed to each city's greater or lesser links to the transoceanic sources of power. At the highest level were the viceregal capitals — Lima, Mexico City, and Rio de Janeiro chief among them; at the next level, the port cities visited regularly by the fleets that provided communication with Europe; then the cities where the high courts called *Audiencias* were located. Finally, all of the other towns and villages of the empire followed in descending order, forming a sort of pyramid. Each city was subordinated to the higher-ranking urban centers that lay nearby, and each extracted wealth from, and provided norms of social behavior for, the rank below. Everyone knew that Madrid, Lisbon, and Seville were located above the apex of this structure, but practically no one ruminated that, at least in economic terms, other European cities like Genoa or Amsterdam might stand higher still.

Incessant conflicts over the geographical jurisdiction exercised by the authorities of one city or another were merely symptoms of struggles to establish or rearrange the pecking order among urban centers. If, as Stanley and Barbara Stein have provocatively asserted, Spain had already begun its decline by the time of the 1492 encounter, so that an Iberian capital like Madrid already functioned as an economic periphery of metropolitan centers in other parts of Europe, then the cities of Latin America constituted the periphery of a periphery.[24] A more rarified situation is difficult to imagine: a huge urban network branching out from transatlantic roots that jealously reserve all political power to themselves but exercise it, apparently, in the service of higher powers, only dimly glimpsed. Our chief interest is the urban culture of Latin America itself, but because it necessarily rested on material foundations we must not overlook economic relationships of dependency. Cultural production was affected at every turn — often decisively — by forces imperfectly understood by people in Latin America, even people in positions of authority, charged with executing orders of obscure logic and distant origin. Local authorities must often have appeared actors in a phantasmagoric shadow play, disconnected from the immediate realities of material life, responding, and appealing for justification, solely to the dictates of the order of signs. Speaking of something as concrete as slavery and other forms of servitude, Braudel has pointed out that they are "inherent in the reduction of a continent to the condition of *periphery,* imposed by a faraway force, indifferent to the sacrifice of men, that moves according to the nearly mechanical logic of a world-economy."[25]

The cultural structures of Latin America floated above this economy, reproducing it in subtle ways. The most lucid minds of the Iberian colonies tried to unveil the hidden workings of the system by seeking its ultimate origins beyond the colonizing metropolis, though their efforts were often condemned by institutional dictates masquerading as public opinion. In his 1624 prologue, Creole author Bernardo de Balbuena shows that his life's work, *El Bernardo,* had an Italian model despite its Spanish subject. Two centuries later, another Mexican, Justo Sierra, suggested avoiding the figurative waters of the "Spanish aqueduct" to draw inspiration instead from French literary sources (the fountainhead not only of modernism but of modernity itself).

Like the huge majority of Latin American intellectuals, both Balbuena and Sierra were men of urban vocation. Both produced the sort of literary texts that served as tacit plans for urban development in an impeccable universe of signs where the ideal city could be imagined into existence — a model of the order that the urban citizenry should strive to incarnate.

2

THE CITY OF LETTERS

 To advance the systematic ordering project of the absolute monarchies, to facilitate the concentration and hierarchical differentiation of power, and to carry out the civilizing mission assigned to them, the cities of Latin America required a specialized social group. Like a priestly caste, this group had to be imbued with the consciousness of its lofty ministry. If it lacked access to the metaphysical absolutes of other priestly castes, this one at least enjoyed dominion over the subsidiary absolutes of the universe of signs, organized in the service of the monarchies beyond the sea. We will call this group "the lettered city."

The universe of signs overlapped the sphere of metaphysics for a long time, and ecclesiastic personnel played an important part as intellectuals until surrendering that role to laymen — professionals for the most part — over the course of the eighteenth century. Two dates signal the two centuries of overlap. The first is 1572, when the Jesuits arrived in Mexico, and the second, 1767, when they were expelled from Spanish-controlled territory by order of Charles III, having already been ejected from Brazil a few years previously. The American mission of the Society of Jesus, according to an early description by the Jesuit father Juan Sánchez Baquero, differed from the mission of the mendicant orders who worked at evangelizing indigenous people. Although they did have some missions among the indigenous inhabitants, the Jesuits sought above all to attend the needs of the white "youths born in this land, with facility and aptitude aplenty, for either good or ill." Because of the idle habits of these young men of privilege, the colony "had neither cultivation of, nor masters in, the exercise of letters" and "the schools were less well attended than the public squares." Sánchez Baquero went on to provide an objective description of the wealthy young men whom he hoped to orient toward the study of philosophy and theology:

> They grow up amid the easy abundance of their parents' houses, lulled by an excessively benign climate, and numbed by constant idleness (venom enough to destroy any great republic, as history teaches). In this land, the scourge of idleness has reached its highest point, because all exercise of arms concluded with the conquest and pacification, and as for occupation in the mechanical trades, it is both inappropriate for such young men (whose just claims to nobility rest in their fathers' deeds or reach back further still) and unnecessary, as well, because of the ready availability of land to provide them with a livelihood.[1]

The educational achievement of the Jesuit order constituted a small but not inconsequential part of the articulation of power in the colonies following the decline of millenarianism among early evangelizers like the Franciscans. The Jesuits trained specialists in the manipulation of symbolic languages to staff colonial administrative and ecclesiastical structures in direct subordination to the metropolis. This administrative function established the norms for urban expansion and determined the material characteristics that framed community life.

The urban centers of Spanish and Portuguese America were fortress cities, port cities, pioneer cities on the frontiers of civilization, but most importantly, they were seats of administrative authority. Within each visible city stood another, figurative one, that controlled and directed it, and this less tangible "lettered city" was not less girded by defensive walls nor less aggressively bent on a certain kind of redemption. The lettered city acted upon the order of signs, and the high priority of its function lent it a sacred aspect, freeing it from subordination to ordinary circumstances and conferring, implicitly, the priestly quality mentioned earlier. The order of signs appeared as the realm of the Spirit, and thanks to them, human spirits could speak to one another. This was the cultural dimension of the colonial power structure, whether or not the people of the time conceived or experienced it as such.

At the center of each colonial city, in greater or lesser scale according to the place of each in the hierarchy of urban centers, nestled a corresponding version of the city of letters to attend to the mechanisms of political power. The viceregal capitals housed a myriad of administrators, educators, professionals, notaries, religious personnel, and other wielders of pen and paper—whom Georg Friederici thought a model of bureaucratic development.[2] From the time of its consolidation in the final third of the sixteenth century, the activities of the lettered city took on huge proportions, apparently unrelated to the tiny number of literate persons who could read its voluminous writings—unrelated, even, to its specific administrative or judicial functions—and the high social rank of its "lettered" functionaries, the letrados, naturally made them large consumers of the colonies' economic surplus. Most of the letrados were involved in transmitting and responding to imperial directives, so they could be found clustered around the royal representatives at the top of the social pyramid.

Three centuries of colonial experience illustrate the astonishing magnitude of this cadre of letrados. To take an example from the field of literature (only one aspect of the letrados' work), the number of poets appears extremely large in all the available sources. Balbuena mentions 300 poets participating in a late-sixteenth-century contest held in Mexico City, and Sigüenza y Góngora collected the work of a similarly large number a century later. The producers and consumers of this literature were largely the same individuals, and their verses moved in a closed circuit that originated in viceregal power and constantly returned to flatter it in flourishes of fulsome praise. This voluminous production—in an ostentatious and exaggerated imitation of contemporary European style—represents the leisured favor-seeking characteristic of viceregal courts in colonial America, since it obviously did not find remuneration in the marketplace. Many scholars have attributed the artistic shortcomings of Latin American colonial literature to the small number of literary artists at work in the colonial setting, but those shortcomings have more to do with the spirit of colonization itself.

Resentful Creoles felt themselves deprived of their just portion of

New World wealth, but contrary to the image of deprivation that they created, the highest levels of colonial society — landowners, merchants, and letrados — absorbed plenty of economic surplus and enjoyed living conditions often superior to those of Spain or Portugal. Here was the "intolerable chimera" of living at the expense of the coerced labor of indigenous people and Africans, acidly denounced by father Mendieta[3] after the appalling indigenous hecatomb that we commonly euphemize as the "demographic catastrophe" of the sixteenth century. At century's end, Mendieta found only a million remaining of the estimated ten to twenty-five million inhabitants of preconquest Mexico. The riches rapaciously extracted from the indigenous population not only allowed the construction of sumptuous churches and convents that still stand in mute testimony to ecclesiastical opulence. Those same riches supported urban Spaniards and Creoles, allowing the letrados the leisure to engage extensively in the splendid epic of Baroque culture.

Various factors contributed to the strength of the lettered city during its early phase. First among them were the administrative requirements of the vast colonial enterprise, as the monarchy multiplied its punctilious — though perpetually and notoriously ineffective — controls designed to safeguard against fraud and abuses. The lettered city derived importance, secondarily, from its centrality to the project of evangelizing and overseeing the transculturation of an indigenous population numbering in the millions. In the universe of signs, the native people could be made to acknowledge, with satisfactory formalism, European values that they embraced only tepidly and may, at times, hardly have understood. The immense tasks of administration and evangelization demanded the soaring numbers of letrados, almost all of whom resided preferentially in urban centers.

But there was a third source of influence accruing to the city of letters. José Antonio Maravall has pointed out that the Baroque period of European history was the first to use mass communications in an attempt to ideologize the masses with full programmatic rigor.[4] There has been considerable debate concerning the degree of influence exercised by the Council of Trent (one expression of this rigor) over artistic expression in the period, but there can hardly be any doubt about the importance and magnificence of the period's official public displays, whether civil or ecclesiastical.[5] In the belligerent atmosphere of the Counter Reformation, both monarchy and church took a militant approach to propaganda and maintained, to that effect, teams of specialists like those to be found in the Holy Office of the Inquisition or in the Society of Jesus. Presented with the huge task of carrying its persuasive message to the colonized masses of the New World, the specialized cadre of letrados took on correspondingly greater operative force, reaching a degree of social importance hardly equaled in all the subsequent history of Latin America. Indeed, the salience of this ideologizing mission finds a European parallel only with the advent of modern mass communications and the development of the mass-culture industry of the twentieth century.

The fourth essential function of the lettered city, already signaled, was the intellectual and professional formation of the Creole elite. In his original request that Jesuits be sent to the New World, Viceroy Martín Enríquez de Almansa referred to the upper-class males who had no need to support themselves — no need even to administer their properties personally — who should be required to direct colonial society in the service of the colonizing project of Spain, maintaining strong ties to the Old World hierarchies of monarchy and church. Looking ahead to the second half of the eighteenth century, we find that the monarchy eventually began to believe that it could carry out its project without the collaboration of the Creole elite, at which point it expelled the Jesuits from its New World possessions and returned the reins of power firmly into the hands of the European-born. During the sixteenth, seventeenth, and early eighteenth centuries, however, the training of the Creole elite remained among the indispensable functions of urban-based letrados.

The crucial social role of intellectuals in this colonizing project has been somewhat obscured by a romanticizing vision of life at the viceregal courts. Interpreters like the nineteenth-century Peruvian writer Ricardo Palma have accented the secretive trivialities of courtly intrigue, providing an entirely insufficient sense of the tremendous influence exercised by letrados in pulpits, universities, and administrative offices, as well as in the theater and various genres of essay writing. Even poets helped construct the ideological framework of Latin American society, and they continued to do so until the vogue of positivistic modernization in the late nineteenth century. Those who considered themselves primarily poets were always a small minority in the city of letters, but a great many wrote amateur verse. Overall, they regarded poetry as part of the common patrimony of all letrados, who were defined essentially by their use of writing, whether in a sales contract, a patriotic paean, or a religious ode.

The power of the lettered city is manifest in its extraordinary longevity. Crystalized during the last third of the sixteenth century, it stood very much intact on the eve of the movements for national independence more than two centuries later. The Baroque style that presided artistically at the time of its origins also proved to be enduring. Regarding the Neoclassical school that eventually displaced the Baroque in Europe, historian and essayist Pedro Henríquez Ureña professed to find in America "very few examples of its influence before the end of the colonial period."[6] Historian Mariano Picón Salas has declared, even more categorically, that the Baroque sensibility permeated the colony, then extended its influence well beyond, at least to the middle of the twentieth century: "in spite of two centuries on enlightenment thought and modern criticism, we Spanish Americans have never managed to escape altogether from the Baroque labyrinth," he wrote. In this he coincided with the Cuban novelist Alejo Carpentier, who even proposed that the Baroque be considered *the* characteristic style of Latin American art.[7] At work here, we can glimpse the conservative influence of the city of letters, relatively static in social makeup and wedded to aesthetic models that kept the letrados constantly harkening back to the period of their collective origin.

So much for the elevated number of letrados, their public preeminence, their social influence, and the impressive resources that they enjoyed. More significant still was the capacity of each letrado to acquire a kind of ownership over his specific corner of the bureaucracy, becoming a petty despot within the larger organization, be it Audiencia, University, or Cathedral Chapter. His is the kind of functional autonomy that Karl Mannheim[8] and, more recently Alvin Gouldner[9] have noticed in their studies of the sociology of knowledge in the contemporary world. Too often, Marxist analyses have cast the bureaucrats as mere executors of the orders issuing from the institutions that employ them. This limited view neglects the letrados's function as intellectual *producers,* who elaborate (rather than merely transmitting) ideological messages, the designers of cultural models raised up for public conformity. We should theorize a more fluid and complex relationship between intellectuals and institutions — and also between intellectuals and social classes. Employed as bureaucrats in the service of absolute monarchies, the letrados came into close contract with the institutionalizing principle that characterizes all power relations. The restricted group of intellectual workers learned the mechanisms and vicissitudes of institutionalized power and learned, too, how to make irreplaceable institutions of themselves. Their services in the manipulation of symbolic languages were indispensable, and therefore the functionaries of the lettered city could assert their own preferences in their work without fearing the loss of their positions. Servants of power, in one sense, the letrados became masters of power, in another.

This heady state of affairs led some — innebriated with the consciousness of their personal influence — to lose sight of their ultimate dependence on the authority of the government. A brief incursion into the nineteenth century will exemplify this tendency and demonstrate the persistence of the colonial mentality. Beginning well before Max Weber's famous studies of bureaucracy, Latin American writers perceptively displayed the letrados' penchant for entrenching themselves within the administrative structures of state power. In the case of Mexico (where the problem remains acute even today), criticism of the "parasitic" bureaucracy intensified during the modernizing dictatorship of Porfirio Diaz in the late nineteenth century. One contemporary man of letters, Justo Sierra, went so far as to write that "the Mexican industry par excellence can be designated by a word well-aclimated in Spanish American vocabularies: bureaucracy."[10] Mariano Azuela dedicated one of his novels of the Mexican Revolution to showing how the bureaucrats of the Porfirian old regime managed to survive the political cataclysm and infiltrate the administrative structures of the post-revolutionary state. If Benito Pérez Galdós called his nineteenth-century Spanish bureaucrats "fish," Azuela outdid him by terming their Mexican analogues "flies." Such criticisms were formulated by Mexican intellectuals who, though they belonged to the city of letters, had not yet been admitted to the charmed inner circle of power — a situation characteristic of the period of modernization and analogous, in a way, to the predicament of late eighteenth-century Creoles struggling individually to replace peninsular Spaniards in positions of colonial administration.

What accounts for the supremacy of the lettered city in colonial Latin America? In this connection, we must recall once more the letrados' drastic exclusivity and strict concentration in urban centers — their natural habitat, so to speak, and one that could hardly exist without them. Only the restricted group of large-scale merchants could equal the urban focus of letrados, and the two groups were often compared. Bernardo de Balbuena's jubilant vision of Mexico City, *Grandeza mexicana* (1604), linked letrados and merchants in a single line of verse: "letras, virtudes, variedad de oficios." And in chapter four of the same work, Balbuena contrasts the uncultured countryside with the triumphant city, emphasizing the urban essence of intellectual life: "[S]i desea vivir y no ser mudo / tratar con sabios que es tratar con gentes / fuera del campo torpe y pueblo rudo." The supreme influence of the city of letters owed even more to its control of the prime instruments of social communication, through which it directed the public dissemination of official ideologies. The two most important intellectuals of colonial Mexico, Sor Juana Inés de la Cruz and Carlos Sigüenza y Góngora, provided apt examples in 1680, when they contributed to erecting triumphal arches to celebrate the arrival of a new viceroy. The themes elaborated artistically in the two arches were, respectively, "An allegorical

Neptune — Ocean of colors — Political simulacrum" and "Theater of Political Virtues." Both themes amply illustrate the ideological function of colonial intellectuals, exemplify the manner in which they sought to conjugate diverse social forces, and typify their constant exaltation of (and quest for patronage from) those, like the charismatic figure of the viceroy, who embodied royal power. This use of art to convey political messages — unsurprising given the social and economic structures outlined in this chapter — was extraordinarily frequent in colonial Latin America, but the phenomenon has yet to attract the critical attention that it merits.[11]

The principal explanation for the ascendency of the letrados, then, lay in their ability to manipulate writing in largely illiterate societies. Amid the grammatological tendencies of European culture in the early modern period, writing took on an almost sacred aura, and doubly so in American territories where it remained so rare and so closely linked to royal authority. During the nineteenth century, when the official influence of Catholicism began to decline, the secondary religion of letters was poised to take its place. Gradually, the universe of signs — of which writing was only a part, albeit a central one — drew on the veneration traditionally accorded it to make itself increasingly autonomous. Baroque discourse bloomed with a profusion of emblems, hieroglyphs, apologues, and ciphers, all commonly incorporated in theatrical displays along with painting, sculpture, music, dance, and decorative use of colors. Letters provided the guiding thread that, according to Goethe, could imbue a potentially chaotic diversity with coherent meaning. The result was a glittering discourse carried forward by a succession of brilliant figures and extended metaphors that animated the whole, filling it with interpretive possibilities. The best examples of this discourse are obviously not the mute texts that we have conserved but in these ephemeral festivals of the arts, best represented by the triumphal arches that commemorated great events.

This symbolic enterprise constituted an abstract, rationalized system, able to articulate its component parts without appeal to anything outside it, drawing only on internal logic of the universe of signs as established, preferentially, by its classic sources. In the late seventeenth century, this network of signs seemed to float autonomously over the material world, a tissue of meaning that overlaid reality, disclosing its existence and granting it significance. The originality and genius of Sor Juana Inés de la Cruz lay precisely in making one version of this gap — that between formal discourse and affective life — into the central theme of her poetry. She seems to have suspected, at one point, that truth inhered principally in the world hidden beneath the tissue of signification and that it welled up frequently and irresistibly from below (like the dreamy irruption in *Primer sueño*) to determine or disrupt the signs, despite their claims to autonomy and self-sufficiency: "Oh vil arte, cuyas reglas/tanto a la razón se oponen,/que para que se ejecuten/es menester que se ignoren!"

The evolution of the symbolic system did not lose momentum with the passage of time, and it seems to have reached its apotheosis in our own era, replete with schemes of signals, indices, acronyms, diagrams, logotypes, and conventional images so many of which imitate, or even aspire to replace, language. The component symbols in each of these systems respond only vaguely to particular, concrete facts of daily life. They respond, instead, to the needs of the symbolic system wherein they were originally conceived, the choice of signifiers being something of an afterthought, indispensable to expression but not essential to their genesis. Their function — founded on reason and instituted through legal mechanisms — is to prescribe an order for the physical world, to construct norms for community life, to limit the development of spontaneous social innovations, and to prevent them from spreading in the body politic. Their profusion in contemporary Latin America lends enduring testimony to the work of the lettered city.

The evolution of the symbolic system is discernable in so many aspects of life that we can hardly mention them all. To trace the contours of the process, let us limit ourselves to one apparently trivial aspect of the larger social phenomenon: street names. At the outset, urban nomenclature drew on the names of people or objects, familiar from daily life and situated in close proximity to the streets in question. For example, a street in Santiago, Chile, was called Monjitas because of the nuns who inhabited a convent on that street. In the second phase, the nomenclature abandons this process of mere metonymic displacement to honor eminent persons or events of significance to the collectivity, so that Rivadavia Street in Buenos Aires or 18 July Street in Montevideo commemorate foundational figures or decisive moments of national independence. At this point, the streets also acquired numerical addresses — odd numbered for one side, even for the other — assigned to each of the existing houses, without taking into account the possibility of future construction. Finally, the nomenclature became more rigidly planned: an abstract system capable of locating a point in the urban grid with precision and simplicity, making exclusive use of numbers in various series (streets, avenues, diagonals), and superseding both the historical names and the homely references to daily life.

The three orderly stages of urban nomenclature were violated in various cities, and the exceptions throw further light on the matter under consideration. In downtown Caracas, people have stubbornly retained a custom whereby the important names are those of the intersections, many of which have historical references (Misericordia, Velázquez, Coliseo). One finds a house or building through reference to its location between two particular named intersections and then through reference to another name, applied to the building itself: the Camoruso Building, Residences El Trebol, and so on. The denizens of this city thus still pay tribute to a past that, nevertheless, has begun to disintegrate (being operative today only in the older sections of town). Bogotá's street nomenclature, on the other hand, is even more precise and rigid than Manhattan's and depends exclusively on numbers, allowing one to know in advance how to find addresses with a precision that includes street, block, and location on the block. The contrast between Caracas and Botogá may appear contradictory, because in most ways Venezuelan society is clearly more dynamic and modernized than Colombian society. The explanation lies in the level of influence exercised by the group of letrados in the development of the two cities: an influence much greater and more strongly articulated in Bogotá than in Caracas (the latter so often shaken by energetic democratizing, antihierarchical movements that presented greater obstacles to the rationalizing action of the intellectual elite).

This is but one example of the highly variable relationship between the larger urban society and the elite city of letters. We can visualize the two cities — the real one and the ideal one — as entities quite distinct yet also inescapably joined. One could not exist without the other, but the nature and functions of each were different. While the lettered city operated by preference in a field of signifiers, constituting an autonomous system, the city of social realities operated in a field of people, actions, and objects provisionally isolated from the letrados' chains of logical and grammatical signification.

In Italo Calvino's beautiful book, *La città invisibili,* Marco Polo tells Kublai Khan about the city of Tamara, where "the eye sees not things but images of things, signifying other things."[12] The dense interweaving of signs imposes itself on the viewer, obscuring all else:

"One's gaze follows the streets as if they were written pages. The city spells out what one ought to think and makes one repeat its discourse, so that what passes for a visit to Tamara is merely a perusal of the names that define it and its components."[13]

Like Tamara, all cities might be considered a discourse articulating double-faced signs in accord with grammar-like laws. Although in some cities the tension between the discursive and material dimensions has become especially acute, all stand as the sumptuous embodiment of a kind of language composed of two different but superimposed grids. The first exists on the physical plane, where the common visitor can lose himself in increasing multiplicity and fragmentation. The second exists on the symbolic plane that organizes and interprets the former (though only for those with a certain affinity and the ability to read as signifiers what others might see merely as physical objects), rendering the city meaningful as an idealized order. There is a labyrinth of streets penetrable only through personal exploration and a labyrinth of signs decipherable only through the application of reason.

This labyrinth of signs is the work of the letrados, or collectively, the achievement of the city of letters. Only the letrados could envision an urban ideal before its realization as a city of stone and mortar, then maintain that ideal after the construction of the city, preserving their idealized vision in a constant struggle with the material modifications introduced by the daily life of the city's ordinary inhabitants.

3

THE CITY OF PROTOCOLS

 By means of the order of signs — organized by rules into hierarchies and classifications of various kinds — the city of letters articulated a specific relationship to Power and provided it with laws, regulations, proclamations, certificates, propaganda, and an overarching ideology to sustain and justify the whole. The letrados affected the majesty of Power and took from it the principles of concentration, elitism, hierarchy, and, above all, the distance that set them apart from the rest of society. And it was this distance — that separated the written from the spoken word, the rigidity of letters from the fluidity of speech — that reserved the manipulation of all legal protocols to the tiny group of letrados.

Tremendous resources were dedicated to the training of the letrados. The first Spanish American university, that of Santo Domingo, was founded in 1538, and others appeared in Lima, Bogotá, Quito, Cuzco, and Mexico City before the end of the sixteenth century. The Crown's attention to higher education (the exclusive province of the lettered city) found no parallels in the area of primary education which would, hypothetically, have benefited a broader clientele. Reading, as well as writing, was practically reserved to the letrados alone, and until the middle of the eighteenth century, ordinary parishioners were forbidden to read the Bible — limitations that stand in stark contrast to the development of primary education and the emphasis on family reading of the Bible in the English colonies to the north.

The exclusive place of writing in Latin American societies made it so revered as to take on a aura of sacredness. The letter was always "obeyed," even when that obedience did not translate into action, whether in the case of royal directives to the colonies or later republican constitutions. Written documents seemed not to spring from social life but rather to be imposed upon it and to force it into a mold not at all made to measure. There was a wide and enduring gap between the prescriptive detail of the law codes and the anarchic confusion of the social realities toward which the letrados directed their legislation. The gap did not reduce the coercive force applied to enforce the legal requirements pertaining to persons and property. Still, the inefficacy of those requirements becomes clear in the monotonous reiteration of identical proclamations or prohibitions in similar edicts issued year after year. Considerable portions of society were somehow able to ignore the legal dispositions of the letrados, as one can discern in an eighteenth-century document decrying the indocile attitudes of early, free-roving gauchos in the Río de la Plata, said to observe no law except for that of their own consciences.

The corpus of laws, edicts, and codes swelled further in the independent countries that emerged from Spanish and Portuguese colonialism, conferring an important role on lawyers, notaries, court clerks, and bureaucrats. The same hands that had documented viceregal prebends and concessions of private fortunes now drew up the legal instruments whereby impecunious new republics contracted public debts or created new private fortunes on lands formerly held by the church. The notaries — recorders of contracts and testaments, wielders of the power to establish or transfer the legitimate ownership of property — maintained, after independence, the same somber preeminence that they had enjoyed in colonial times. Incessant disputes over property titles lent salience to lawyers as well. Notaries and lawyers knew the requisite legal phraseology, almost invariable for centuries, perpetually indispensable for the official sanction of ownership and the long-term preservation of wealth.

Nor were notaries and lawyers the only ones for whom rhetoric and oratory constituted essential professional instruments. Medical doctors were frequently trained as intensively in the literary arts as in human anatomy and physiology. Referring to the medical school of Bahia, Gilberto Freyre pointed out that even in the scientifically oriented nineteenth century "medical science found itself, at times, reduced almost to becoming a hand-maiden of classical literature, oratory, or rhetoric; secondary to elegance of expression, less important than correctness and grace in speech or writing, undervalued in debates that turned more on grammar than physiology."[1]

The exaltation of writing — initiated during the colonial period and stubbornly maintained after independence — created a characteristic situation of diglossia,[2] whereby Latin Americans exhibited a sharp and habitual distinction between two separate kinds of language. The first of these was suited to public, formal, or official occasions, laden with courtly formulas of peninsular origin, its Baroque mannerisms carried to an unparalleled extreme. This sort of language served for civic ceremonies, religious liturgy, and the careful protocol of exchanges between members of the lettered city. Above all, it served for writing, and it was practically the only language to find its way into the written record. The other half of Latin American diglossia was the informal speech of everyday life, the version of Spanish or Portuguese used by the poor and unpretentious with each other on all occasions and employed by almost everyone in private. This popular language appears quite rarely in writing, most often when some irate letrado wrote to inveigh against its clumsiness, its jabbering informality, and its unfettered innovation (equated with ignorance, corruption, and barbarism). In the dichotomous division of colonial society, this vernacular corresponded to the so-called *plebe,* a word referring in an undifferentiated way to the mass of common people, whether Mexico City beggars, Argentine gauchos, or the caboclo peasants of the Brazilian backlands.

Whereas everyday speech evolved constantly, absorbing all kinds of contributions and distortions and developing a myriad of regional variations, the official public language was characterized by its rigid conservatism and general uniformity from place to place. Popular speech tended to appropriate many formal locutions as one can observe from those preserved in the rustic language of isolated regions, but the flow of borrowings did not normally run the other way. The purity of the formal, written language was jealously guarded, and only great social upheavals could forcibly open it, piecemeal, to the syntactic and lexical creativity of informal speech. The letrados' fervent adherence to courtly peninsular norms, later institutionalized by the Royal Academy of the Spanish Language, can be properly understood only by visualizing them as a tiny minority ever on the defensive against the unlettered throng that made up the immense majority of the population.

The embattled city of letters was hemmed in by distinct groups, the first of which spoke at least some kind of Spanish. Immediately surrounding the letrados were the lower and middle sectors of urban society: downwardly mobile Creoles and Europeans, along with all the inhabitants of darker complexion, including blacks, indigenous people, and those of mixed blood. An excellent illustration of the letrados' attitude toward this urban plebe can be found in the following late seventeenth-century description by Carlos Sigüenza y Góngora, the pre-Enlightenment intellectual often considered the most advanced of his day: "[A] plebe so extremely plebeian as to be the lowest of the low, composed of Indians, blacks (born in America or in various African nations), all sorts of mixed breeds (mestizos, mulatos, moriscos, chinos, zumbaigos, lobos), and also Spaniards who (content to be called scheming, good-for-nothing, capesnatching rogues) abandon their obligations and become the worst scum of all."[3] Nevertheless, it was among such "inferior" people, the majority of the urban population, that a new, American version of Spanish emerged during the first centuries of colonization, despite the determined resistance of the letrados.[4]

A second, much more numerous group encircled the lettered city a bit farther out, beginning in peripheral neighborhoods like the indigenous quarters of Mexico City and sprawling across a countryside dotted by great estates, little villages, and hidden camps of runaway slaves. Indigenous and African languages predominated in this second besieging ring during the early phases of colonization, and the letrados regarded it as enemy territory. One of the most frequently repeated appeals to the king—long resisted by the religious orders but finally imposed during the reforms of the eighteenth century — was that he oblige the indigenous people to speak Spanish. For the Spaniards who settled in American lands and for their descendents, land ownership and tribute labor privileges guaranteed a high living standard, free from manual labor, but their cultural dominance depended on their use of language. Together, language and property defined the local ruling class. Centuries later, when the white descendants of the conquerors began to lose their monopolistic access to wealth, they began to produce mountains of writing with a panicky urgency that clearly indicates the importance of language as their remaining claim to social dominance.

Possession of particular varieties of language thus crystalized a social hierarchy, defining the preeminence of those at the top and clearly marking a defensive perimeter between them and the threatening lower classes. The defensive posture of the letrados intensified their adhesion to the linguistic norm,[5] as defined by Coseriu, which in this case could be none other than the peninsular norm, more specifically, the norm established by usage at the royal court, the absolute center of political power. The conquest of new lands forced the peninsular tongue to incorporate words for new plants, animals, and social customs,[6] but these lexical additions did nothing to alter the normative outlines of the system. Peninsular norms continued to provide an ideal model for all individual linguistic acts, and if this model initially betrayed the regional diversity of the colonists' Iberian provenance, it became increasingly fixed by the formulaic style of the imperial bureaucracy and also, for the better-educated among the letrados, by the literary style of peninsular belles lettres. Among the peculiarities of colonial life, few are more noteworthy than the influence of the documentary umbilical cord that carried imperial orders and provided linguistic models for letrados in the far-flung dominions. Whatever else they transported, the ships plying the Atlantic always arrived laden with written messages, pronouncing on the most sensitive matters of colonial life. Royal directives elicited lengthy, elaborate replies that advanced counter-arguments point by point, making the official missive — along with official reports and chronicles — into a literary genre in its own right.

An intricate web of epistolary communication covered the American domains of Spain and Portugal. The letters were copied three, four, ten times to be sent by different routes in the hopes of assuring the safe arrival of at least one. Nevertheless, they were often intercepted and constantly glossed, contradicted, or forwarded with rebuttals and accompanying evidence as appendices. The entire network was controlled from its external pole (Madrid or Lisbon), where the documents pertinent to any particular matter were gathered, the information assessed, and the issues resolved, resulting in further orders sent across the Atlantic in a pack of new letters. The job required a (frequently ambulatory) corps of notaries and scribes and, in the administrative centers, an active bureaucracy—a swarm of letrados who circulated through the system, adapting themselves to its norms and contributing to their diffusion.

Vaca de Castro, whom the Spanish king sent to pacify Peru in 1540 after the Almagro rebellion, may not have been a valiant military man, but he was an effective letrado who used the system of written communication as his deadly instrument. The letter that Vaca de Castro sent to Charles V from Quito on 15 November 1541, upon learning of the murder of Francisco Pizarro, includes the following evidence of his epistolary labors:

I wrote immediately to the town council of Cuzco and to various private parties, and also sent a copy of the orders whereby Your Majesty made me governor, authenticated by two notaries, along with testimony of how I have been received here in that capacity with attendant powers. I wrote Captain Per Alvarez Holguín, who has 150 men in the area of Cuzco preparing for an exploratory expedition; and then I wrote to Lima, sending copies of the dispatch by four separate routes, with letters for the town council and others, such as Gómez de Alvarado and other persons of quality, who used to take their side but have since turned against them. I wrote to don Diego and also sent spies to write or come tell me what is happening in that city; soon I should have replies. And I wrote to the towns on the coast and to various private individuals there, as well, securing them all in the service of Your Majesty.[7]

Vaca de Castro himself became a casualty of the system, however, when another official intercepted letters that the unfortunate letrado had sent to his wife about the treasure that he was busily accumulating behind the king's back.

"Language is the companion of Empire" according to the often-quoted phrase from Nebrija's *Gramática sobre la lengua castellana* (1492), the first grammar of a romance tongue, and the city of letters defined itself by its manipulation of that minority (sometimes almost secret) language. To defend its purity was the primary mission of the letrados, the only way of keeping open the channels that linked them to the metropolis and sustained their own power. Thus the letrados, though generally greedy, were also generally more loyal to the Crown and more devoted to its service than other groups — such as the religious orders or secular clergy — who likewise formed part of the imperial project.

The elaborate forms of courtesy that developed during the colonial period (and are still regarded as traditional elements of Spanish American culture) derived originally from the usage of the royal court at Madrid. They crossed the Atlantic and were incorporated into the public registers of speech as part of late sixteenth-century mannerism, thereafter becoming paradigms of elegant expression assiduously aped by the social groups that surrounded the inner circles of power, imitated even — with ingenious malice — by picaresque figures like Cervantes's characters Rinconete and Cortadillo.

Another result of the letrados' penchant for exclusivism was the obsessive linguistic purism that has characterized American society since early times. This relentless purism has produced (in the scheme established by Ferguson) a "high variety" of language closely linked to peninsular, courtly norms and quite divergent from the diverse regional "low varieties." Thus, we find in the spoken language the same kind of disjuncture already noted between the legal protocols of the letrados, on the one hand, and messy social realities, on the other. Linguists agree that, by the time of independence, the *vosotros* form of the second person plural had already been supplanted in the speech of educated (as well as uneducated) Spanish Americans by the more hierarchical *ustedes* form.[8] Nevertheless, in 1830 Simón Bolivar conjugated second person verbs in the obsolete *vosotros* form when composing his last proclamation, and a century and a half later, school children all over Spanish America still practiced the conjugating the same form, although it had acquired in their ears an utterly stilted and theatrical ring, inappropriate to normal speaking or writing.

Conservative linguistic purism went somewhat out of style during the late nineteenth-century period of "modernization," but another heritage of the letrados' long tenure remains very much in place: educated people's use of two parallel and semantically equivalent vocabularies, one more prestigious and formal than the other. The letrados became translators, appealing to a metalanguage in order to move back and forth between these the two lexical codes. One can take examples of such exercises in translation from the letter written by Sigüenza y Góngora to explain a rebellion that had taken place in Mexico in 1692. The Mexican letrado used the word *elotes*, then provided a translation for the benefit of his reader in Spain: "green ears of corn." He mentioned *zaramullos* and then had to explain what they were: "good-for-nothing, cape-snatching rogues."[9] Whether vulgar or, perhaps, exclusively Mexican, these expressions evidently required explanation for an overseas reader. The very existence of parallel lexical codes implied alterity.

The *costumbrista* (local color) novels of the late nineteenth century resorted to glossaries of regional vocabulary for similar reasons, since they sought an audience in other Spanish-speaking countries, particularly in Spain itself. Indeed, one might say that the same forces were operative in the mid-twentieth century, leading Alejo Carpentier to use some rather curious arguments to make the case that the Baroque style was quintessentially Latin American:

The word *pino* is sufficient to show us a pine; the word *palmera* is enough to define a palm. But the word *ceiba* — naming an American tree that Cuban blacks call "the mother of trees" cannot bring that gigantic trunk before the eyes of people from other latitudes. . . . That can only be accomplished through the apt deployment of various adjectives, or, in order to avoid the use of adjectives, by the metaphorical use of nouns to take their place. If one has luck — literarily speaking, in this case — the purpose will be achieved. The object will come alive; it will be viewed and hefted by the reader. But the prose that gives it life and substance, weight and measure, is a Baroque prose, necessarily Baroque.[10]

Obviously, it is not words but cultural contexts that permit the reader to *see* a pine, a palm, or a *ceiba* in literature. While European writers could address their audience without worrying about the marginal readers outside of Europe, writers like Carpentier, from other regions of the world, continued to yearn for European readers and regard their reading as the true and authorizing one. What Carpentier proposes is the absorption (into the work's narrative language, though not without leaving some trace) of the explanatory metalanguage that bridges the gap between the two lexical codes described above. His proposal certifies the continued sense, on the part of some twentieth-century Latin American letrados, that they remain exiled on the fringes of a civilization whose animating center lies in the metropolitan powers of Europe.[11]

This example helps demonstrate how the lettered city defends the norms — cultural as well as linguistic — of the metropolis where the literature admired in the marginal zones is produced. Both norms are rooted in writing, that not only determines the status of diglossic "high varieties" of the spoken tongue but also engulfs the entire sphere of acceptable linguistic expression. Such norms clearly contradict the habitual usage of language in large illiterate communities. All attempts to deter, defy, or negate the imposition of these functions of writing must, inescapably, also be formulated in writing. One might go so far as to assert that writing eventually looms over all human liberty, because new emerging groups can effectively assail positions of social power only on a two-dimensional battlefield of line and space.

The history of graffiti in Latin America, at least, offers some substantiation for this view. Because it is written on a wall, because it is frequently anonymous, because its spelling is habitually faulty, and because of the kind of message it transmits, graffiti attests to an authorship outside the lettered city. The writers of graffiti — in their expressions of denial, protest, even desperation — frequently reveal their lack of familiarity with the conventions of written culture. Three examples, drawn from the history of Latin America at two-century intervals, offer proof of the persistent, rising hegemony of writing.

The first comes from the sixteenth century, when the plunder of the Aztec capital gave rise to bitter disputes and clamorous protests on the part of certain captains among the Spanish conquerors who believed themselves unfairly slighted in the distribution of the booty. Bernal Díaz del Castillo, who was one of them, has told the story sagaciously and in detail: "And as Cortés was at Coyoacán, lodged in palaces with whitewashed walls, easy to write on using charcoal or other "ink," morning always dawned to reveal insulting phrases, in prose or in verse, written there during the night . . . and some used words not fit to put in this account."[12] Each morning, Cortés wrote his replies in verse on the same wall until, infuriated by the insistence of his interlocutors, he closed off the debate with these words: "Whitewashed wall, a fool's stationary." Cortés thus reestablished the hierarchy of writing—that ought to be reserved for superior purposes—and condemned graffiti because anyone could produce it. Graffiti was to remain a clandestine appropriation of writing, an illegal attempt to subvert one of the ordering principles of society.

In the eighteenth century, a postal inspector named Alonso Carrió de la Vandera expressed similar reprobation upon contemplating graffiti on the walls of inns where he stayed during a trip to Alto Perú, present-day Bolivia. By the nature of the messages and the clumsiness of the writing, Carrió de la Vandera discerned that this graffiti was the work of "low-lifes." The graffiti testified to the writers' desire to exist more completely by leaving a tangible mark of identity: "In addition to the obscenities that they write with charcoal on the walls, there is no table or bench without the first and last name of one of these fools carved upon it."[13] The derogatory description, "fools," occurs again. Only "fools" write with materials that society did not reserve for that purpose. In *El lazarillo de ciegos caminantes* (1773), Carrió de la Vandera recorded impressions of his trip from Buenos Aires to Lima, and he frequently encountered expressions of oral culture, such as the songs of the early gauchos, entirely alien to the province of letters. These expressions had arisen spontaneously in the countryside, in the outskirts of towns, in the lower strata of society, far from the normal channels of writing. But well before the late eighteenth century, they had already begun to find their way into writing through the medium of graffiti, in two variants that maintain their vigor, as we well know, until the present day. First there is the record of repressed sexuality that found its favorite venue on the walls of bathrooms and latrines. More than by a person's hand, these obscenities seem written by a penis escaped from captivity. Then, there are the names graven by knives in indelible letters — striving thereby to achieve a more permanent embodiment of self — that now decorate virtually every public monument.

In the third quarter of the twentieth century, we have all been witnesses to the invasion of a third type of graffiti, the political slogans that covered the walls of Latin American cities in those years. Here again, the thirst for liberty flowed into clandestine writing, done rapidly at night to escape official vigilance, obliging the forces of repression to become whitewash brigades and to limit other uses of writing, as well — confining the power of letters to even narrower channels governed by even more stringent norms. Amid the nation-wide agitation of 1969, the Uruguayan government prohibited by decree the public use, in any context, of seven particular words. Surely the authors of the measure understood that by banning the words they did not eliminate what the words described. Their intention was to fulfill the most esteemed function of the lettered city by keeping order in the universe of signs, preserving its univocal semantic fixity and social exclusivity. Control of the written word's channels served the purpose admirably, as Colombian journalist Daniel Samper Pizano pointed out at about the same time: liberty of the press had been reduced to the liberty to buy a press.

The city of letters would like to be as unalterable, as atemporal as the order of signs, in constant opposition to the material city whose existence is merely historical and therefore bound to the ongoing transformations of society. Conflicts between the two were inevitable, and the critical problem would be the letrados' capacity to adapt themselves to those social transformations. Hence, let us inquire about that process of adaptation, about the function of the lettered city in changing times, and more particularly, about its ability to survive political revolutions by reconstituting and restoring its fractured foundations on new ground.

The great model, in this regard, lies in the wars of independence that began in 1810 and established a paradigm repeated with variations during the successive waves of revolutionary change that have swept over the continent since then. As late as the mid-twentieth century, the resilient permanence of the letrados during the Mexican Revolution obsessed writer Mariano Azuela and figured importantly in his novels, from *Andrés Pérez maderista* on. If Azuela found the process of revolutionary change chaotic and irrational, he found the letrados' ability to harness its social energies and turn them to their own benefit truly mesmerizing.

The independence and its aftermath demonstrated three important points. First, it revealed the degree of autonomy achieved by the city of letters within the larger power structure and its intellectual availability in the face of menacing transformations. No person illustrates this point better than does the precursor of Colombian independence, Antonio Nariño, who was still a royal bureaucrat when he privately published his Spanish translation of the *Declaration of the Rights of Man* (1794). This document was ideologically key to the Creole resistence — strongly manifested a few years earlier, in Nariño's part of the continent — against the efforts of Spain's Bourbon monarchs to tighten their imperial control. Next, the process of independence showed the limitations on the letrados' action, limitations associated with their dependence on royal power to regulate the hierarchical order of society. As that beleaguered royal power disappeared, the letrados enlisted in the patriot cause discovered that the majority of the Spanish American population (blacks, mestizos, mulatos, and indigenous people) in fact leaned toward the royalists, forcing the patriots to offer social concessions. From Simón Bolívar's early move to free slaves in 1816 to subsequent measures extending juridical equality and citizenship to the members of indigenous communities, such measures proved disastrous to the supposed beneficiaries, who had correctly "considered the king to be their natural protector against the overweening aspirations of the Creoles, lords of great estates, avid for inexpensive labor." But that is another story.[14] Finally, the aftermath of independence indicated the letrados' capacity, not only to adapt to change, but also to keep that change within certain limits, gradually reining in political movements that had temporarily escaped from their control, reasserting their influence over the rebellious masses and over the self-aggrandizing opportunists among their own midst as well. Antonio Nariño, in his "Discurso en la apertura del Colegio electoral de Cundinamarca" (1813), again provides an apt example. After reviewing the marvelous expectations that had accompanied the early project of independent federalism, unanimously recognized as democratic and just, he concluded that all had been devoured by the voracious appetites of functionaries who used federalism merely as an ideological cloak for demands to advance their bureaucratic careers, thus culminating the quest for public employment that had set Creoles and peninsular Spaniards at loggerheads during the final decades of the colony. "Three years have gone by," wrote Nariño in 1813, "and nevertheless no province has a mint or money in its treasury, or schools and roads, or armed forces, gunpowder, and cannon. All they have is a considerable number of functionaries that consume the little revenue that remains and defend the new system with all their might because it favors them."[15]

The letrados thus acted as an "adjustable bridle," its reins slipping easily from the hands of viceroys into the grip of the newly powerful *caudillos,* the generals on horseback who replaced the liveried servants of monarchy in the aftermath of independence. Now, the task of the city of letters was to draft new laws, edicts, regulations, and above all, constitutions for emerging independent states. Eventually, they would attack the vaster challenge of fashioning systematic legal codes. Once again, the function of official writing began to create an idealized political architecture, "an airy republic" in the acerbic expression of Bolívar, detached from reality, prolonging the same disjuncture between social life and legal structures that had existed during the colonial period. The inhabitants of the lettered city multiplied, though there were limits on their increase. The substitution of peninsular-born letrados by their Creole counterparts had produced a significant turnover of administrative personnel, and the expansion of state institutions — especially with the creation of legislative bodies — far overreached the new nations' puny economic resources amid the general penury of the first decades after independence. Nor were there schools to train the new letrados, and the unanimous call for *education* rivaled the clamor for *liberty* during these years — education not for the sake of economic development (that became stagnant and even lost ground during this period), but because the organization of an educational system was indispensable to the political and administrative order.

It is highly revealing that public debate in the young republics often addressed linguistic matters, and especially, forms of writing. Overall tendencies still favored the cultivation of legal formulas and protocols, though the growth and the changing composition of the city of letters, in the process of reconstituting itself after the social cataclysms of revolution and war, had some innovating impacts. One was the bankruptcy of Latin, assiduous labor of Jesuits prior to their expulsion, bereft now of the colonial splendor that produced Rafael Landívar's *Rusticatio mexicano* and a thick bundle of other American writings. The obsolescence of the letrados' secret language is marked by the publication of the first true Latin American novel, *El periquillo sarniento* (1816), by the Mexican author Joaquín Fernández de Lizardi. In his preface, Lizardi wavers between two potential audiences, one old and one new, but he inclines finally to the new one. Therefore, "to save less well-educated readers from the stumbling blocks of Latin" he decides to "put the Castilian translation in place of it, sometimes putting the original text in notes, other times leaving only the citation, and sometimes omitting even that."[16] At the same time, the speech of the streets erupts into Lizardi's text, bringing with it a vocabulary that until then had never entered the realm of public writing, never left its mark on the decorous paper of printed books and gazettes, but did so now with an exuberant delight that Lizardi's moralistic disclaimers did little to disguise. It is significant that Lizardi moved away from Latin and toward popular speech in criticizing "bad judges, criminal notaries, crooked lawyers, shiftless physicians" who were all necessarily letrados.[17] In fact, far more than is usually recognized, the entire corpus of writings published by Lizardi under the pseudonym of "Pensador Mexicano" constituted a direct challenge — less to Spain, the monarchy, or the church than to the lettered city as a whole. The novelty of Lizardi's work derived from a situation that was itself new: the existence of a group of letrados who had failed to gain entrance into the powerful inner circles of the city of letters despite their ardent desires to do so.

Like the anonymous writers of graffiti before him, Lizardi realized that he had to challenge the lettered city on the battlefield of writing. Unlike them, he could seek the attention of a newly literate, bourgeois public. While graffiti represented an individual, illicit, and almost predatory appropriation of writing (still tightly monopolized by the letrados in the eighteenth century) the nineteenth-century literary production of the Pensador Mexicano was built on a marginal but expanding social base. The new periodical publications of the day were purchased by readers who did not form part of the power elite but whose literacy and ability to pay offered writers like Lizardi an alternative to the sort of support from wealthy patrons that had been typical earlier. "To whom, in all justice, should one dedicate one's labors," wrote Lizardi, "if not to those who pay to read the results with their own money? They are the ones who foot the printer's bill and are consequently the surest Maecenases [patrons]."[18] Unfortunately for the Pensador Mexicano, however, his project was premature and condemned to fail because this market remained too narrow. Like Balzac, whose potential market was far more powerful for a number of reasons, Lizardi eventually came to lament his "lost dreams" of artistic autonomy.

Liberty, in effect, had been absorbed by writing and was impossible without it. The great Latin American educators of the period — Andrés Bello, Simón Rodríguez, and later, Sarmiento — all understood this, and it animated their almost obsessive concern with the problem of spelling reform. Facilitating access to writing was a central purpose, but so was creating a system that functioned consistently according to the most rational possible norms. Their concern for orthography curiously parallels the urge for spelling reform that had accompanied the creation of Spain's absolute monarchy centuries earlier. The drive to standardize had been, in that case, intensified a hundredfold by the need to administer a vast empire. Witness the publication of a series of orthographic treatises running from the well-known one by Nebrija (1517) to that authored by López de Velazco (1582) — significantly, head of the Council of the Indies — before the first Spanish American speller, that of Mateo Alemán (1609), appeared in Mexico.

With the foundation of independent states after 1810, Latin American letrados who assumed responsibility for creating national educational institutions faced a similar problem of standardization, though with some subtle differences. The earlier Spanish reformers had essentially transcribed the linguistic norms defined by usage at the royal court and made them the obligatory written vehicle of administration over distant regions of the empire. The spelling reformers of nineteenth-century Spanish America, on the other hand, were altering that previous norm to close the gap between everyday American speech and the ossified written language assiduously preserved by generations of letrados. That gap presented a pedagogical problem, since it made writing more difficult to learn for speakers of the ordinary American idiom, but there was also a higher theoretical purpose for undertaking orthographic reform. Independence in matters of writing would complement the political independence already achieved and lead to the creation of a national literature. Not everyone saw it in the same terms, however. In Buenos Aires, Juan Cruz Varela argued for a national literature but viewed it exclusively as a product of the letrados. "The press is the only vehicle fit to communicate the production of human genius," he wrote in 1828, and he proposed a return to "good Spanish writings" of the peninsular variety as a means of preserving the language.[19]

Simón Rodríguez, Bolívar's influential tutor, conceived of political and literary independence in broader and more original terms, postulating a parallelism between government and language. He maintained that the two must be in harmony and that therefore they must be coordinated. Rodríguez insisted, furthermore, that both government and language must be the native, idiosyncratic expressions of American society and not merely European imports. Thus, he proposed that "words be drawn with signs that represent the mouth" in order to reflect American pronunciation, which had grown far different from the pronunciation of Madrid, and he also proposed that new republican state institutions derive organically from the components of American society and not from a mechanical transplantation of European institutions. Rodríguez argued that spelling follows three principles — reflecting a word's origin, its normal written usage, and the spirit of those who speak it — and that the third principle (pronunciation, essentially) should make the spelling "conform to the mouth when neither origin nor usage decide." He then astutely extended the argument by analogy to "the art of drawing republics," in opposition to what he saw his contemporaries doing in 1828: "[W]hen neither origin nor usage decide, they make recourse to the third principle, but instead of consulting the spirit of Americans, they consult that of Europeans. Everything is imported."[20]

No less than Lizardi, Simón Rodríguez aimed his barbs at the city of letters, but his campaign, like that of his contemporary, Lizardi, was doomed to failure because of the letrados' remarkable capacity to weather the revolutionary storm and reconstitute their power in the independent republics. Rodríguez reasoned that one did not make republics "with writers, with literati, with doctors of law" but with citizens, and further, that the task of forming citizens was doubly urgent in a society that the colonizers had never prepared for that purpose. "Nothing is as important as forming a People," he wrote, "and that should be the chief occupation of those who undertake the social cause."[21] In the writings of Rodríguez during the two decades between 1828 and 1849, one can trace the gradual foundering of an educational project that not even his admiring disciple Simón Bolívar could regard, amid the multitudinous urgencies of the organizational morass that followed independence, as more than a generously conceived but utterly unviable utopia. Rodríguez reserved his sharpest criticisms for the process of educational restoration that he witnessed during his lifetime. Disconsolately, he observed the erection of a system primarily destined to produce bureaucrats, perpetuating an antidemocratic concentration of power and resulting in a ruling elite like that of the colony:

Do not expect from these schools something that they cannot give. . . . They are turning out letrados, not citizens. Make up your minds that the graduates will sally forth, books and compasses under their arms, to greet with "vivas" anyone whom they believe inclined to give them the public employment upon which they, or their fathers, . . . have set their hearts.

From the way in which education is conducted today, we can count on men to occupy lofty stations and supply civil, political, and military leadership — but all three areas will lack a rank and file or will have to struggle perpetually with untrained recruits.[22]

Because he was an ardent follower of Bolívar, aware of the difficulties that embittered the Liberator's final years, Rodríguez saw clearly that the letrados had made their own revolution under the cover of larger revolutionary transformations associated with independence. The self-aggrandizing success of the lettered city would hobble the true reformers, and it would quickly bend to the ambitions of the caudillos. Rodríguez feared that the function of the letrado class was "to cut all communication between the people and their representatives, or to twist the meaning of measures that cannot be conveniently concealed, . . . or to exalt the idea of sovereignty, thereby raising and exploiting the excitement of the people."[23]

Therefore, Rodríguez proposed a social education for all the people and extended to them the double rights of literacy and property that had formerly been the exclusive possession of the colonial ruling class and were now to be the patrimony of all citizens — a radical, democratic vision rooted in the thought of Rousseau. The vision of Simón Rodríguez was also enriched by his conception of American societies as quite different from European ones, constituting a distinctive variant within Western culture or (in Enlightenment terms) within the universal category of mankind. For that reason, his emphasis on writing and spelling reform did not aim merely at advancing literacy, as was the case with another leading educator of the period, Andrés Bello. Instead, Rodríguez sought to inculcate an "art of thinking" by coordinating the universality of modern reason with the particularities of American thought through the language that Spanish Americans learned in infancy.

But the project of Simón Rodríguez, like all the orthographic reforms inspired by the spirit of independence in Latin America's new republics, ultimately failed, giving way after a few years to the reimposition of norms established by the Royal Academy of the Spanish Language in Madrid. The weakness of the reform projects themselves and, occasionally, their excessive attention to trivial detail, may partly explain this failure. More important, however, was the failure of the larger social project of which spelling and literacy composed only a part. The new nations of Latin America had failed to construct democratic, egalitarian societies, and their educational institutions, instead of producing an informed citizenry, turned out custodians of the traditional, hierarchical social order. The pedagogical dreams of the Liberator's tutor were distinguished not by their impact but by their exceptional egalitarianism and by a determined utopian spirit that his writings still communicate today, as if confidently awaiting their eventual realization.

In his article "Extracto sucinto de mi obra sobre la educación republicana," published in 1849 in Bogotá's *Neo-Granadino,* Rodríguez presented the gist of his philosophy of social education, enunciated earlier in his "friendly advice" to the Colegio of Latacunga, Ecuador. In these writings, he plainly indicated the secondary role that he assigned to "reading, writing, and arithmetic" — subjects that had been practically the only concern of primary schools, even the new Lancasterian schools that Rodríguez despised. Rodríguez assigned the primary role in education to the cultivation of reasoning ability, which he saw as the cultural foundation of republicanism, not unlike the "living logic" of Carlos Vaz Ferreira half a century later.

Reading should be the last step in the work of education. The order should be: calculating, thinking, speaking, writing, and *then* reading, rather than reading, writing, and counting, as is done everywhere now, with logic left to the few lucky enough to attend secondary schools. Those few emerge spouting syllogisms, vomiting paralogisms and sophistries by the dozen in everyday situations. If they had learned to reason as children, taking familiar propositions as logical premises, they would not be so full of deceit. Despite their learning, they would not reason thus: a) The Indian is not what I am; b) I am a man; c) Therefore, he is a brute and must be beaten into working.[24]

Rodríguez had an interest in prosody that derived from his attention to the speech of ordinary, illiterate people, and through it he manifested his anti-letrado attitude and his rejection of the conventional emphasis on legalistic formulas in writing. Common speech might exhibit frequent pronunciation defects and barbarisms (which Rodríguez, no less than Andrés Bello, sought to correct), but it also functioned as a system of communication in which all speakers spontaneously produced intonation and rhythm appropriate to their meaning. "All people are prosodists in conversation, however poor their pronunciation, but when reading they go back to the monotonous tones of the classroom and put their listeners to sleep."[25] Simón Rodríguez thus took a pre-Saussurian (or anti-Derridian) position on the relationship between reading and writing, one that recognized "an oral tradition independent of writing and set in a very different manner."[26] His ideas in this regard, traceable to Rousseau's *Essay on the Origins of Languages,* led the republican educator to attach supreme importance to speech and, consequently, to the phonetic resources that contribute to oral communication as a system of signification. To him, reading was "the resuscitation of ideas buried on paper" and the most important aspect of education was helping children to achieve the precision of expression required to make language an effective instrument of thought:

Consider the importance of correcting errors early; of learning to pronounce, articulate, and properly accent words — acertaining their meaning, ordering them in sentences, and giving them the emphasis appropriate to their sense. Consider the importance of finding the appropriate expression for each idea, of understanding rhetorical figures and matters of number and tone. This is what instructors should teach, because children think, speak, persuade (and persuade themselves).

For all of this, they must make calculations, and if they err, it is because they calculate using erroneous information.[27]

More than an art of writing, Rodríguez was proposing an art of thinking. This is demonstrated by the ways that he expressed his ideas on paper, using diverse kinds of lettering, paragraphing, bracketing, and numbering systems in order to represent the structure of his thought graphically. Like Vaz Ferreira, though more schematically, Rodríguez strove to devise a rigorous, rational transcription for the mechanism of thought. There is nothing here resembling the sentence structure, discursive style, or essay organization typical of Latin American prose in the first half of the nineteenth century. Rodríguez removed writing from its normal patterns, purged it of rhetorical adornment, extracted its essences, and boiled them down to their most laconic expression, then distributed them, textbook-style, on the page so that the reasoning process and its component concepts would be accessible to the eye. In effect, his theory of pedagogy did something similar to what Mallarmé did with poetry later in the century. If the life of Simón Rodríguez showed his social and political opposition to the lettered city, his original approach to the transcription of thought illustrated his energetic rejection of the conventional written formulas and protocols of his day, even if, like the writers of graffiti, he had to resort to writing in order better to combat its pervasive power.

4

THE MODERNIZED CITY

 The onset of modernization around 1870 was the second test facing the lettered city in the nineteenth century. Modernization posed even stiffer challenges than had the process of independence, but because of the widening of literacy in the period, it was also richer in possibilities for the letrados.

Once again, as had been the case in the wake of independence, existing power structures were challenged by social sectors recently incorporated into the privileged circle of letters, and letrados, especially the doctors of law, became targets of criticism in a variety of venues — from the popular periodicals published in Mexico by Antonio Vanegas Arroyo (and often illustrated by José Guadalupe Posada) to the broadsides and dime novels on gauchesque themes appearing in the Río de la Plata. Many intellectuals joined in the critique, particularly the new generation of educators who, without having read the work of Simón Rodríguez, carried on the tradition of anti-letrado pedagogy that he had pioneered earlier in the century. Thus, in his book *De la legislación escolar* (1876), Uruguayan educational reformer José Pedro Varela assailed the national university's concentration on producing law degrees. "As a class," he wrote, "lawyers are not better than other professionals — not more moral, nor more just, nor more selfless, nor more patriotic — only more presumptuous and more backward in their thinking."[1] Varela attacked lawyers because they belonged to the class "of those who talk, who formulate laws, and cover reality with gilded rhetoric." For him, university graduates exemplified the gap between the city of letters and urban realities. Instead of faithfully representing or interpreting those realities, they *gilded* them.

With perspicacity greater than that shown by José Martí (who in 1891 spoke of "artificial letrados," incapable of understanding the "natural men" on whom the caudillos—supposedly more in tune with social realities—built their dictatorships) Varela saw that the doctors of law had been able to graft themselves comfortably on to the trunk of caudillo power. "The spirit of the university accepts this order of things," wrote Varela, "reserving to itself privileges and honors that it believes to be great victories, while leaving the rest of society to languish under a despotic government."[2] This was the criticism that the new rationalist—and soon, positivist—camp leveled at the accommodation reached by the city of letters during the half century following independence, as Liberal and Conservative intellectuals alternated in power, eventually creating the liberal-conservative amalgam described by Colombian writer José María Samper in 1862.[3]

The way to combat the lettered city and reduce its abusive privileges, according to the influential formulations of Spencer, Pestalozzi, or Mann, was to recognize the incontestable dominion of writing and to facilitate access to literacy by new social groups. That is the origin of the educational reforms that spread throughout Latin America after 1876, the date of Varela's own initiative. The period also witnessed progressive transformations of the university, as the incorporation of positivist technical education tempered the hegemony of law and medicine. On the statistical graphs of the last quarter of the nineteenth century, two steep upward curves—representing export and demographic expansion, respectively—account for the demand for technical education. Neither of these could equal the vertiginous growth of urbanization,[4] however, as "almost all the capital cities of Latin America doubled or tripled their population in the fifty years after 1880."[5] After a lapse of several centuries, the former outposts of empire were finally making effective their original mission of imposing an organizing imprint on the surrounding rural areas.

These were cities "primarily conceived as bureaucratic centers, [and] commerce and industry had almost no part in their formative period," in the words of Chilean historian Claudio Véliz, who goes on to explain that the urban population was primarily "employed in the service, or tertiary, sector of the economy and included domestic servants as well as lawyers, teachers, dentists, civil servants, salesmen, politicians, soldiers, janitors, accountants, and cooks."[6] A considerable part of the tertiary sector was composed of intellectual activities, and these activities now became more diversified. Administrative, legal, and political personnel had to share the prestige of letters with practitioners of three rapidly growing activities that absorbed a large number of letrados and established a constant demand for new recruits: education, diplomacy, and journalism. Only journalism enjoyed substantial economic independence from government coffers, and, with the exception of a few major daily newspapers and illustrated magazines, most periodical publications remained predominantly political in orientation, as had been the Romantic tradition. Thus most journalists received their most important compensation in the form of political spoils — i.e., access to public employment or elected office in the wake of partisan victory — so that, in practice, their independence from the state had narrow limits. Even so, journalists did enjoy a new autonomy from the state when compared with the earlier letrados, and educators did also, especially when the system of public schools expanded beyond the close supervision of the highest spheres of government. The public prominence of the burgeoning tertiary sector (calling attention to itself with the showy habits characteristic of the nouveaux riches) has been interpreted by some historians as evidence of the sector's excessive growth and voracious appropriation of public resources. It is not clear, however, that its expansion proportionally exceeded the explosive economic growth of the period.

On the other hand, there can hardly be any doubt of the social prestige that accrued to intellectual activities in the modernized city. The ideals and myths of modernization continued to make the position of the letrado among the most respectable and admired — if not necessarily the best remunerated — on the urban scene. Thus young women of the lower middle class dreamed of attending normal school and graduating as teachers (like the *"maestra normal"* depicted in the fiction of Manuel Gálvez), while illiterate but prosperous ranchers and immigrant shopkeepers dreamed of a university degree for their sons (as in the drama *M'hijo el doctor* by Florencio Sánchez). Letters seemed to offer a ladder for the upwardly mobile, conferring respectability and access to the centers of power, as well as a greater relative autonomy regarding those centers of power, thanks to the new diversity of sources of wealth and the broadening economic base of the period's developing bourgeois societies. The literate could now sell scripts to theatrical companies or articles to newspapers, be employed as reporters, work as teachers, compose lyrics for popular music, or write or translate for the penny press. This last activity became considerable enough, by the end of the nineteenth century, to lead to the creation of copyright laws and organizations charged with collecting the royalties owed to member authors. The independent exercise of the "liberal professions" (as they were still called at the time) and the creation of institutes (such as those bestowing titles to primary or secondary school teachers) presented other opportunities for intellectual laborers. Those who occupied these positions found themselves less dependent on the government and therefore freer to foster a critical spirit, sometimes incorporating the perspectives and demands of the urban lower classes. Nevertheless, the ambition of the new letrados generally included, with obsessive insistence, their own personal infiltration into the inner circles of power, still viewed as the primary origin of privilege, position, and wealth.

The limits of the letrados' incipient autonomy can be sensed in an examination of the social myths that entered the urban folklore of Latin America at about this time. The most intense were the myths of the countryside brought to the cities by the migrating rural people who swelled the poor, peripheral neighborhoods of capital cities all over the continent. As the process of modernization advanced and generated riches, for the most part on the backs of the peasant masses, the resulting rural banditry and messianism lent prominence and energy to the mythic figures of rebel and saint. The poor of city and countryside revered both bandit and messiah as Romantic symbols of resistance who defied the unjust social order. Revealingly, both are solitary figures emblematic of the isolation and limited associational solidarities of rural society. Still, they took hold in the cities and have continued to flourish there to the present day.

Along with myths recently established in the cities as a result of rural-urban migration, toward the end of the nineteenth century one can also detect the emergence of other myths, urban in origin. These were much weaker than those already mentioned, however, and a comparison with the United States, where such urban myths developed far more vigorously, aptly illustrates their relative weakness in Latin America. Even the Río de la Plata area, the recipient of large-scale European immigration like that flowing to the United States, did not resemble the United States in this respect. Darcy Ribeiro has observed of Argentina that "the descendants of the immigrants have not yet managed to put their stamp on the national ideology,"[7] and his meaning becomes evident if we evoke the extraordinary diffusion of U.S. pioneer myths that gave prominence to frontiersmen like the cowboy heroes of so many thousands of dime novels in the late nineteenth century. Immigrants were a part of the frontier experience in the United States, where many of them were rewarded with land. Although the expansion of the Argentine frontier ("the conquest of the desert") closely paralleled the westward advance of the frontier in the United States, it was carried out by the landed oligarchy and the army, restricting access to newly incorporated land and paralyzing the democratic function of spontaneous pioneer migrations that occurred on the North American frontier.

The same democratizing recognition of individual effort, external to — and even opposing — the power of the state, also fed the growth of urban myths like that of "the self-made man" in the United States. In the field of letters, this mythic impulse expressed itself in two heroic and solitary figures: the small-town newspaperman who successfully denounces the abusive corruption of the powerful and the trial lawyer who clears the name of his client, falsely accused by rich,

Machiavellian schemers. Despite overwhelming evidence of the extraordinary concentration of power that has occurred in the United States, these urban myths, in which writing plays a central part, continue to nourish the U.S. popular imagination. Why did neither develop in Latin America? Their absence indicates that, notwithstanding frequent imputations of anarchic Latin American individualism, individual Argentines, Brazilians, or Mexicans have little faith in their ability to confront and overcome the enormous weight of institutionalized power.

Myths start from something real, but they constitute more wishful thinking than accurate depictions of the way that things really function. If myths condense collective desires about the world, then in the case of the United States they gain wide play from positive perceptions of the capacity of the individual, while in the Latin American case they rest on an acute sense of individual helplessness in the face of monolithic state power. In other words, Latin American urban societies model action more collectively and their social myths configure opposition in terms of groups: spontaneous protests, mass demonstrations, multitudinous demands. The myth of a unified peasant-worker-student movement, so central to the discourse of the left (and especially of student activists) since the early twentieth century, is the product of an urban literate culture, with clear antecedents in Europe and without equivalents in the United States.

Thus, the larger historical experience of Latin America delineated the realm of the possible when, toward the end of the nineteenth century, a dissidence began to manifest itself within the lettered city and to configure a body of critical thought. There were many causes for this dissidence — among them, a sense of impotence and frustration felt by intellectuals whose numbers had risen out of proportion to the real opportunities offered by Latin American societies, echoing the experience of colonial Creoles confronted by overweening Spanish power, and forcing many to seek employment in more developed countries. The modernizers' critique of Latin American reality was shaped by cultural forms that, however modernized they might appear, still largely fit a traditional mold. Vaz Ferreira once remarked that those who lived too late to be positivists became Marxists instead — highlighting the way that Latin American intellectuals have selectively adapted successive European doctrines to their own vigorous, internal traditions. If they did not adopt the individualistic Romanticism of Germany, but instead embraced the social Romanticism of France and made Victor Hugo a hero in Latin America, it was because the French version dovetailed more neatly with the collective emphasis of Latin American culture. Analogously, the positivist sociology of Comte and Spencer gained such enormous influence here not only because of its explanatory force but also because it meshed well with our mentality, providing a persuasively modern and universal social analysis that nevertheless reenforced a traditional emphasis on groups and classes and permitted a continued focus on a closed regional context.

In spite of the admonitions of Simón Rodríguez, the spirit of colonization continued to hang heavy in the air, and the dissident critique of the modernized letrados ultimately reproduced many central principles of the lettered city. Most important was the persistent association between the world of letters and the exercise of power in society. However much they formulated an independent current of opposition thinking, the dissident letrados attacked the traditional concentration of power only tangentially. They directed their criticisms at those currently in control, trying to supplant them and the philosophies they espoused, rather than trying to alter the exclusive contours of the system. A slogan from colonial times — "Good king, bad government" — seemed to guide the mechanisms of opposition, as it has continued to do ever since in some countries, Mexico being a notable example.

Of all the ways in which the exercise of letters broadened during the period of modernization, the early-twentieth-century expansion of the press had the widest and most obvious repercussions. The press was the direct beneficiary of the educational reform laws that had extended literacy to new sectors of the population. As Arnold Toynbee observed of England, the immediate result was a spate of opportunistic and often sensationalist publications. In Buenos Aires, one might mention the newspaper *Crítica* (Botana, 1913), although the most enduring success went to the major newspaper enterprises (for example, *La Nación,* also of Buenos Aires, or Brazil's *O Estado de São Paulo*) that became pillars of the modernized system and bastions of the lettered city. To the contrary of what the selfless pedagogical reformers had expected, the legions of new readers boosted the consumption of newspapers and magazines far more than they expanded the market for books. If educational reformers like José Pedro Varela had hoped to shake the foundations of the lettered city, the overall impact of their reforms was to broaden and strengthen those foundations, only enhancing the prestige of writing and other symbolic languages in the exercise of power. Sarmiento, perhaps the most famous reformer of an earlier generation, had foreseen this effect and made it an explicit part of his reform project, while Varela and the young reformers of the later nineteenth century had hoped for a democratizing challenge to the city of letters.

Eventually, if they lived long enough, the members of the modernizing generation became coopted into the circle of power during one or another of the twentieth century's social and political transformations. The personal evolution of Mexico's Justo Sierra provides an example. In 1878, in the pages of his student newspaper *La libertad,* he lashed out at "those man-made marvels called abstract constitutions," dubbing them "the dense fantasies of those who devise social and democratic codes," and contrasting them to "the practical approach in which rights and duties, in their real, human dimensions, are the products of need, interest, and utility."[8] Yet, it would be this same Justo Sierra who, after long efforts, managed to have the university (always the most precious jewel of the lettered city) reorganized on a new basis, conferring upon it an explicitly sacrosanct quality called "autonomy," to which José Vasconcelos, another reformer, added a motto whereby the voice of the university spoke for nothing less than the Spirit of the Race.

In 1918, young rebels at the University of Córdoba advanced similar demands for academic autonomy in Argentina, presenting the university as properly the guiding organ of the social body. It was a typical strategy of upward social mobility on the part of a new sector or class making its bid for power. The university continued to offer a bridge by which to cross into the city of letters, as it had earlier to socially ascendant groups throughout the nineteenth century, when its main function had been to train bureaucrats, legislators, and government ministers. Now the university was to operate in a wider field of endeavors, participating in the processes of modernization and national integration. Amid a reigning climate of agnosticism, the academy took on many of the functions that had once pertained to the established church. Looking beyond the arguments of the Cordoban university reform, with its intensely democratic ideology, we can perceive at stake a change of personnel and doctrine but never a threat to the privileges of the lettered city, which emerged strengthened by new letrado professions that integrated the middle class into the existing system. Doctors of law would now have to share their power with sociologists, economists, and educators, but they retained functions primary to the city of letters, especially the elaboration of law codes.

In their task of writing laws, the lawyers received the collaboration of another specialized group, the philologists, whose traditionalist orientation helped compensate for the disorienting effects of democratization. For example, the astonishingly prolix *Réplica* that Rui Barbosa presented to the Brazilian senate in 1902 as his answer to the Civil Law Code under consideration by that body was not the selfish caprice that many have alleged. To the contrary, Barbosa's reply fully embodied the historical function of the lettered city and would have profound repercussions in Brazilian jurisprudence. Invoking the Benthamite equation of legal certainty with unambiguity, Barbosa argued that "a civil code must be an exceptional work, a monument to the culture of its age" because "more than a scientific task, it is a great expression of national literature," and therefore its prose must be rigorous and clear, avoiding all possible misreadings.[9] The rigid semantic system of the city of letters found complete vindication in legal codes and constitutions, which required the most unequivocal language possible. A univocal interpretive system (that strove to permit one reading only) had to be based on the linguistic principles cited by Simón Rodríguez: etymological origin and constant, long-term usage. Inevitably, however, methodical pursuit of these two principles directed attention to linguistic traditions and cultural links with Portugal and Spain. Turn-of-the-century Latin American philologists helped maintain the already habitual traditionalist tone of the lettered city and their contribution to the process of modernization thus subtly offset it in some ways.

National languages were the most effective instruments for disciplining the symbolic order of national cultures, so the modernizing process that began around 1870 was accompanied by the creation of official normative bodies, patterned on the Spanish Royal Academy and charged with standardizing each country's particular variant of Spanish or, in the case of Brazil, Portuguese. In their conception and initial organization nearly all of them embodied an explicit recognition of ancestral ties with Iberia. Beginning with the Colombian Academy, founded in 1872, all the Spanish American academies (with the exception of Argentina) originated as "correspondents" of the Spanish Royal Academy. The Argentine Academy was founded simply as a confraternity of writers, perhaps to stake greater claims to cultural autonomy in the most economically dynamic country of the region. Brazil, another of the region's most dynamic countries, also eschewed direct ties to the former colonizing power and, in the sagacious assessment of Manuel de Oliveira Lima, was "dedicated more to the future Brazilian language than to the past Portuguese language."[10] The appearance of these academies constituted the response of the lettered city to the linguistic subversion occurring as a result of general democratizing trends, aggravated in certain countries by massive immigration and complicated everywhere, among the educated, by the overpowering influence of French culture. There was also concern that American Spanish was becoming excessively fragmented along national lines. "We are on the verge of becoming separated," wrote Rufino José Cuervo of Colombia, "as occurred with the daughter [languages] of the Roman Empire." The academies that were founded to repel these threats were, for the most part, ineffective, but the generation of trained Latin American linguists associated with them nevertheless produced a splendid set of philological studies. The Colombian Academy, possessing the best linguistic team on the continent, was more successful than most — no doubt partly because it had a more direct connection to the government. Miguel Antonio Caro, the founder of the Colombian Academy, actually became president of his country.

During the period of modernization, two other great projects necessarily fell to the city of letters. Both were operations that demonstrated the autonomy of the order of signs — its capacity to structure vast designs based on its own premises, partially escaping the particularities and conjunctures of living reality. One, considered later in this chapter, concerned the ingenious diorama of the urban landscape, whose dynamism continued somewhat to encumber the independence of the signs, as we have seen. The other operation involved the surrounding vastness of "nature" and the rural folk cultures that had been developing on their own for centuries.

For the first time in its long history, the city of letters was making a determined effort to integrate and dominate entire national territories, to domesticate Nature and subject rural cultures to the modernizing norms of capitaline society. Early in the nineteenth century, in his "Allocution to Poetry" (1823) — asking it to leave Europe and take up residence in America — Andrés Bello had proposed two great American themes: Nature and History. But only history attracted wide attention from Latin American poets in the ensuing years and, the sumptuous descriptions of José María Heredia notwithstanding, their treatments of Nature remained mostly cosmetic imitations of the European schools from which they were copied, without the authentic accent attained by their treatment of other, heroic or amorous, themes. Despite insistent proclamations of the Romantic literary project, and despite the importance that the fertility and exuberance of its natural environment has always held in the imagination of outsiders, nineteenth-century Latin America could not boast artistic expressions of the theme equivalent to those in the United States: the transcendentalism of Ralph Waldo Emerson's *Nature* (1836), Henry David Thoreau's *Walden* (1854), or Herman Melville's travel writings; the brilliantly illuminated landscape paintings of the Hudson River School, from Thomas Cole and Albert Bierstadt to Frederic Church. In fact, it is Church to whom we owe splendid South American landscapes not undertaken by local painters, busy with bourgeois portraits and epic scenes of military pomp and heroism. If anything illustrates the innately urban spirit of Latin American culture, it is this artistic detour around the continent's natural splendors, normally obligatory stops on any Romantic tour. Characteristically, the Venezuelan poet Antonio Pérez Bonalde chose to sing the praises of nature at Niagara Falls, and the enthusiastic prologue to his *Oda al Niágara* was written by José Martí, who lived fifteen years in the United States, where he belatedly absorbed the influence of the transcendentalists and penned admiring articles on Emerson and Whitman. Martí was unusual in his tenacious defense of natural themes, even as they rapidly lost favor everywhere toward the end of the nineteenth century. During the course of that century, no Latin American Thoreau went to inhabit the solitude of nature and write a diary about its glories. Latin American writers lived and wrote in cities and, if possible, capital cities, remaining resolutely urban people, however much they sprinkled their works with the naturalistic details required by the literary vogue of local color.

Given their urban tradition, they could fairly easily convert Nature into a symbolic diagram, a cultural model where urban society could read, not so much the nonhuman world, as its own problems, projected as absolutes. The two greatest Latin American poets of the period of modernization, Rubén Darío and José Martí, did just this, though somewhat differently, in their respective structures of literary signification — Darío's more deceptively aesthetic, Martí's more dramatically realist.[11] There remained another problem, however, in this project of incorporating the city's rural surroundings: the cultural production of rural people (themselves presumably "natural," since they lived in nature). Their language, poetry, narrative, worldview, historical experience, and long-standing traditions — in short, all their principal symbolic constructions—were embodied in an orality with peculiarities not easily reducible to the normal systems of urban communication.

Much like a naturalist novelist, in his prologue to *El gaucho Martín Fierro* (1872) José Hernández gives a detailed description of his research on the people and social customs that he depicted in his book. He concludes with his insistence on portraying "as faithfully as possible, with all his peculiarities, that original social type of our pampas—so well-known as such, and frequently so erroneously judged, that he is difficult to study—who is well on the way to disappearing altogether because of the rapidly advancing conquests of civilization."[12] Here, the best known and most determined defender of the rural culture of the Río de la Plata from the destructive onslaught of liberal modernization proposed, by way of methodological considerations, two concerns that subsequently proliferated in so-called "gauchesque" literature and, more broadly, in works representing rural culture at about this time throughout Latin America. The first concern—that the approach be faithfully realistic and scientific—denotes, by its very emphasis, the distance between the investigator and the object of his observation. Clearly, the two belonged to different worlds, corresponding to the old formula of civilization versus barbarism, though rural people were here no longer being called barbarians. The second, complementary concern was that the species under scrutiny had reached the verge of extinction, making the undertaking analogous to anthropological studies intended to salvage the vanishing cultures of primitive peoples. The investigative powers of civilization were to be applied to a cultural universe believed doomed because incapable of adaptive evolution.

To the degree that this dying cultural universe depended on unwritten traditions and oral communications, one might say that urban letters came to its rescue, but only to hold its funeral services in writing. The efforts of Hernández, like those of most *costumbrista* writers of the period were symbolic encodings at the service of, and intended for, a literate, urban audience. Only the huge and unforeseeable success of *Martín Fierro* situated it on the boundary between the literate and illiterate communities of Argentina. While many read the book, even more *heard* it read or recited and, thanks to its verse form, fixed it in memory, where it remained relatively impervious to the sorts of transformations usually affecting oral tradition.

Modernization brought similar operations to other, widely separated parts of Latin America, since rural cultures were everywhere withering, to one degree or another, under the extending influence of urban civilization, and everywhere urban intellectuals hurried to collect endangered oral traditions. Their efforts — though obviously generous and useful — also illustrate the general outlines of the problem, as writing collected the splendors of oral traditions in peril, precisely, because of writing. The living memory of the songs and narratives of rural tradition was being destroyed by the cultural substitutes emanating from the cities, by the urban educational standards they promoted, and by the ever-expanding circuits of the written word. In this sense, the books of letrados like Hernández entombed oral production, immobilizing and fixing forever a phenomenon normally characterized by permanent transformation — reshaping, in the process, a material essentially antithetical to the individualized rigidity of books.

Of oral culture it is especially true, as Lévi-Strauss observed of myths, that all particular versions constitute variations on the same underlying themes. This insight recognizes, not only the adaptation of oral production to different concrete circumstances, but also the presence of historical processes operating within it. Such processes are difficult to measure in the myths of tribal people, but their presence is easily confirmed in the verbal inventions of peasant cultures, as the somewhat atemporal currents of tradition conform to the larger historical circumstances that impinge upon rural lives. In spite of the well-known conservatism of rural cultures (owing to the slow tempo of their evolution) and in spite of their attachment to the lessons of the elders (derived from a system of education that grants precedence to the wisdom of experience), these cultures were never immobile, nor did they ever stop producing new values and artifacts. Rural cultures did not reject the transformative effect of the new.

They integrated it, instead, into the continuum of tradition, constantly rearticulating that tradition by selecting, discarding, and recombining its components to produce responses appropriate to the changing historical context. One could argue that this is not radically different from the process of change in urban culture, though in the latter case the modifications occur more rapidly and the elements are substituted in quicker succession. Above all, the products of urban culture undergo a more demanding individuation. Literate society sharply distinguishes individual expressions within the general cultural flow, abstracting them from it, raising them to a higher level, classifying them by genre according to various formal requirements. The resulting products are called works of literature.

In the Brazilian half of South America, the task of compilation (segregating and limiting the oral cultural continuum) fell to Sílvio Romero, an intellectual of ardent modernizing spirit, a man imbued with the thought of contemporary Europe's various scientific schools, ranging from Gervinus, Buckle, and Curtius, to Scherer and Schmidt. Romero sought to master the scientific theories and methodologies of his time and to apply their rigor and efficiency to the collection and classification of Brazilian oral literature[13] in his "Estudos sobre a poesia popular no Brasil" (appearing the *Revista brasileira*, 1879–80), *Cantos populares do Brasil* (1883), and *Contos populares do Brasil* (1885). The Romantic faith in "the infallibility of the people" (the words are those of the philologist and collector of folk tales, Jacob Grimm) was replaced, in the work of Romero, by the methodical, scientific analysis of a material that has been separated from its cognitive function in the life of a community as part of its transformation into literature. As André Malraux said, the gods enter art museums as nothing more than statues.

The spread of costumbrismo and the realist novel throughout Latin America obeyed more-or-less scientific precepts similar to those applied by Romero. Costumbrista and realist authors based their work on the same positivism that defined an overall division of labor in the economic and social structures of modernization, assigning entire countries different functions in the international economy and casting individuals in specialized social roles. For the interpreters of oral tradition, the division of labor delimited their specific field of study and fixed it within an analytical grid that further ordered and classified the contents. As a result, national literatures were constructed for the first time in Latin America, somewhat belatedly, following lines organized earlier by European Romanticism. One sign of the times was the appearance of the first Latin American literary histories (by Sílvio Romero in Brazil, and by Francisco Pimentel in Mexico) that wove heterogeneous and often unorthodox threads into webs of a shape predetermined by the needs of emerging nationalist projects.

Latin America thus recapitulated a process that had occurred half a century earlier in Europe, under the influence of different methodological perspectives but in response to the same Romantic propositions (i.e., the importance of folk traditions in national identity) and, at least partially, in response to the same socioeconomic conditions (e.g., the consolidation of a bourgeois order). The concept of *literature,* with its ability to forge a national spirit, gradually replaced the concept of belles lettres as interpreted by Louis de Bonald and Madame de Stael. Thus, in its new specificity, literature was constituted as an autonomous field of knowledge as a consequence of — or, at least, enhanced by — the humble oral productions of rural cultures whose long history and conservatism provided a broad legitimating foundation for conceptions of nationality. Predictably, it was in Brazil, where literature had contributed in the most clearly articulated manner to the constitution of a national identity, that recourse to oral tradition was first made. Soon, however, Romero's lead was followed by Ricardo Rojas in Argentina, another writer in the vanguard of a nationalist tide that swept over the entire continent in the early twentieth century. The timing of the phenomenon is explained, not only by the advent of new concepts and categories of classification, but also by the death throes of many traditional rural cultures, which spurred and facilitated the collection of specimens for national literatures. In the words of one critic, "nineteenth-century costumbristas . . . responsible for the collection and preservation of such material were activated by this sense of imminent loss even when they also resigned themselves to its inevitability."[14] The general context is summed up by a historian in the following manner: "Progress as conceived and implemented by the elites tended not only to impoverish but to deculture the majority. As the folk culture lost to modernization, the options for the majority diminished."[15]

The creation of national literatures and national histories toward the end of the nineteenth century constituted a major triumph of the lettered city. The proliferation of the written word permitted the letrados to discipline the countryside, imposing homogeneity and social hygiene, and into the emerging concept of literature were incorporated many materials extraneous to the educated elite's earlier concept of belles lettres. Literature absorbed the multiple contributions of traditional rural culture and articulated them with other elements into a discourse on the definition, formation, and collective values of the nation. In function, then, the literary discourse strictly paralleled the impetuous production of Latin American historians who, in the same period, used their writings to glorify patriotic heroes, placing them above partisan factions and making them symbols of a national spirit. In search of a usable past, late-nineteenth-century historians also began to dissolve the sense of a clean break with the past that earlier Neoclassicists and even Romantics had attributed to the wars of independence, enabling a reinterpretation of the colonial period as the cradle of national experience. The pioneering work of Brazilian historian Capistrano de Abreu provides a notable example. Finally, historians came to value past expressions of the localist and regionalist spirit of the common people — and even, though timidly, the phenomenon of racial mixing — as contributions to emerging national identities. Above all, historians bound the disparate threads into a unified narrative of order and progress, a story of the gradual maturation of the nation, structured to advance the purposes of centralized power.[16]

The imposition of writing subjected the production of rural culture to urban norms but obviously failed to eliminate it entirely. The deculturation of the countryside associated with the process of late-nineteenth-century modernization actually opened the way for new patterns of rural culture, mixtures of orality and writing, strongly marked by the historical circumstances in which they emerged. But the lettered city remained largely blind to this generation of new cultural idioms, which were urban as well as rural and which developed particularly in popular music and theater.

The letrados' appropriation of oral tradition concluded in an exaltation of political power at the national level. This was clearly the objective of the lectures that Leopoldo Lugones gave to the assembled members of the executive branch of the Argentine government, collected and published three years later in his book, *El payador*:

I entitle this book with the name of the errant troubadors of old, who crisscrossed our country singing their ballads and laments, for they were the most significant figures in the formation of our race. Just as has happened in all the other branches of the Greco-Latin trunk, that formation began here, too, with a work of great beauty, and its primary agent has been poetry, inventing a new language for the expression of the new spiritual entity — that of the soul of the race in formation — and creating, thereby, the fundamental distinctness of the *Patria*.[17]

It is a nostalgic and idealizing manifesto emphasizing the commonplaces of patriotic rhetoric: "errant troubadors singing ballads," "the Greco-Latin trunk," and "the soul of the race" — all intended to evoke the spirit of the *Patria*. Elsewhere in the prologue to *El payador,* Lugones reveals the real social entity against which his discourse is deployed. They are the lower-class immigrants whose presence in the city and whose capacity for oral and written cultural production could hardly be denied:

The throng from overseas, like ungrateful beggars raising a ruckus at the doors of our houses, unleashed against me their mulatto accomplices and their mestizo devotees. They approached me with solemn expressions, these vulgar masses, trembling with rage and protected by parliamentary representation, savoring for an instant the chimerical pleasure of disgracing a writer immune to the prurient temptations of universal suffrage.[18]

This "throng from overseas" had already begun to produce their popular one-act farces, and they contributed in diverse and uneven ways to shaping a musical and poetic expression of overwhelming influence in Buenos Aires, the tango. The vitality of the tango in the period when Lugones delivered his lectures, its intimate connections with the city's plebeian culture, its insouciant tendency to straddle the division between colloquial orality and clumsy writing, its distance from urban high culture, and, more than anything else, its uncontainable popularity, made it impossible to incorporate immediately into the rigid parameters of the lettered city. Not until its mid-century decline would the tango be captured by writing and co-opted into a quasi-official urban mythology.

The challenge of the tango and its eventual neutralization exemplify the second great operation performed by the lettered city in the period of modernization. Even more arduous and delicate than the appropriation of rural orality was the containment of changes in the urban landscape. The concentration of population in the peripheral neighborhoods of Buenos Aires paralleled the concentration of political power in the city center, creating a tense and unruly agglomeration of social forces that seemed constantly to threaten the kind of eruption that would surely subvert the hierarchical structures of urban life. Once again, the principal challenge to the supremacy of the city of letters emanated from the city of social realities, its constant and indocile companion. Vertiginous urban growth and the advent of mass society sowed consternation among the ruling groups. This was especially so in the Atlantic port cities with large black or immigrant populations, since the internalized influence of the church still tempered subversive impulses in the Pacific-coast countries of large indigenous population.

Beneath its mask of liberalism, the period of modernization depended on a system of intensified repression. Its effects were worse in the countryside than in the city, because it channeled to the lower sectors of the urban population, and especially to organized workers, at least some of the benefits derived from the period's incipient industrialization and its burgeoning import-export trade. These small concessions to the volatile urban masses were possible thanks to the more drastic repression of the rural poor. Even more effective in meeting the challenge from below was the expansion of public education that occurred primarily in cities and offered prospects of upward social mobility. Because the leadership of workers' organizations shared the urban perspective of the intellectuals and had imbibed the basic modernizing assumptions of the time, they tended to accept the government's repressive policies in the countryside. In this sense, the rural anarchism of the Flores Magón brothers in Mexico was exceptional in Latin America. Therefore, urban radicals tended to applaud the educational expansion of the turn of the century as an advance toward equality despite its general neglect of rural people. Only later, around 1930, did the frustration of their expectations lead urban intellectuals, labor leaders, and political voices of the lower middle sectors to take up the grievances of the countryside — including those of indigenous people and blacks — and unfurl the banner of agrarian reform to rally support that would help them address demands and grievances of their own.[19]

Long before that development, the chief cities of Latin America had begun to change physically in response to the formidable internal and international migrations that gathered there, totally overwhelming the existing urban infrastructure. Perpetual snarls in communications and transportation resulted not only from the rapid population growth, but also from the increasing demands created by the port cities' intermediary function in the booming import-export trade. For the first time in Latin America, urban people witnessed the sweeping transformation of their material surroundings as the colonial architecture of their youth disappeared, to be replaced in a fraction of a single life span by an utterly different cityscape. Thus, around the turn of the century many Latin American cities recapitulated the Parisian reforms promoted by Baron Haussmann a generation earlier, leading Baudelaire to remark that Paris was changing more rapidly than could the human heart.

Although it meant little to fresh arrivals from the countryside or from overseas — to whom all was unaccustomed and for whom nothing in their new environment represented history and identity — the dissolution of the familiar urban setting produced a powerfully disorienting sense of uprootedness for longtime inhabitants of Mexico City, Buenos Aires, or Rio de Janeiro.[20] Incoming migrants, because of the very fact of their migration, had already accepted the idea of change and lacked emotional attachments to their new surroundings, but older residents felt cut loose from their past and hurled willy-nilly toward the transformations of a precarious future, and the literature of the period, written primarily by the descendants of traditional families, tends to reflect their point of view. Conflict between the two groups sometimes surfaces here in the form of xenophobia. For the most part, however, the problems of urban transformation brought by economic modernization affected immigrants and old-stock residents alike. The extreme mobility of urban society, the bustling crowds of strangers, the new customs and social mores, the successive waves of demolition and construction that followed one another in an accelerating rhythm — all suggested instability, loss of the past, and a future to be conquered. The city no longer lived for a yesterday fondly remembered and rich in signs of shared experience. Instead, it lived for an unpredictable but fervently imagined tomorrow. Unrelenting astonishment, day in and day out, was an exhilarating but trying experience for urban dwellers.

Once again, in a salvage operation precisely parallel to the one undertaken for the oral traditions of the countryside, the written word came to the rescue. Just as *costumbrista* writers had used elements of rural culture to create persuasive national identities and to found national literatures, they performed a similar operation for the cities. Supposedly, they set about reconstructing the urban past, but they did so at the service of the present, so their reconstruction surreptitiously incorporated — and thus legitimated — the shifting norms of the modernized city. While the rural past had offered roots of nationality, the urban past was to provide touchstones of collective identity among city dwellers. In both cases, the task was to instill an arrogant pride in the authentic heirs of certain luxuriantly idealized ancestors and to force the humble newcomers from abroad into accepting such admirable progenitors as their own. In sum, the written word designed the foundations of national identity and constructed a version of it in peoples' minds, all in the service of a particular political project. As anyone who stopped to reflect might have observed, this critically important process depended on pen, paper, and graven images — on words braided into discourses, printed and spoken. Less substantial, but even more crucial, was what occurred in peoples' minds: the dreams that these written materials led them to conceive, as the page dissolved into reveries before their eyes, exciting their imagination, unleashing and channeling the force of their desire.

Therefore, the late nineteenth century witnessed a veritable super-production of books telling what cities were like before the era of modernization. Among the better known examples, one could mention: for Lima, *Tradiciones peruanas* by Ricardo Palma; for Mexico City, *México a través de los siglos* by Vicente Riva Palacio; for Santiago, *Recuerdos del pasado* by Vicente Pérez Rosales; and for Buenos Aires, *La gran aldea* by Lucio V. López. On the surface, they are simple nostalgic reconstructions of what once was and is no longer, the recreation ("so that they do not die altogether") of vanished settings and customs. Consequently, these books represent the application of Goethe's precept, whereby "the only thing really ours is what we have lost forever." However, a more probing investigation reveals — predictably, because all texts are determined by the situation in which they are written — that the perspective of these books was structured by the social context and ideology of modernization. More than recuperate the past, they invent a particular version of it. It is a move impelled by the experience of losing cultural roots and seeking new ones, certainly, but also by the search for a new set of all-inclusive social norms.

As the *real* city was destroyed and then reconstituted on a new basis, the city of letters found the opportunity to encode it anew in words and images. This new encoding involved the unfettered play of desire much more than the deposition of facts and figures, which mostly function to provide the resulting ideological constructs with the convincing texture and colors of reality. The ideological function of these representations of the urban past emerges even more clearly when one considers the complementary elaboration, occurring at the same time, of representations of the urban future. The larger world of Western letters, influenced by utopian thinkers such as Robert Owen and Saint-Simón, had already produced some key texts (Edward Bellamy's *Looking Backward* and William Morris's *News from Nowhere,* for example) as well as many attempts to found utopian

The Modernized City   71

communities, very frequently aimed at the "new continent," just as in the Renaissance.[21] Nevertheless, the freest flights of the imagination are probably the dream cities of what Rimbaud correctly called *Les illuminations*. Interestingly, the great writers of Latin American high culture evinced scant enthusiasm for the elaboration of utopian visions, and they left that activity largely to amateurs. In the case of Uruguay, for example, the writing of utopia was left to an auctioneer (Francisco Piria, *Uruguay en el año 2000*) and to a painter (Pedro Figari, *Historia Kiria*).

Cities of the past and future were equally constructions of the imagination, fueled by desire, induced by the disintegration of familiar urban surroundings around the turn of the century. Unlike the cities of the future, the cities of the past could be embellished with the discourse of nineteenth-century realism, but it would be imprudent to read the descriptions of old Montevideo, Rio de Janeiro, or Mexico City as historical fact. It is more appropriate to read them as responses to rapid, disorienting social change and as efforts to establish cultural models for a new age. Their fundamental message lies not in the evocative details but in their overall discursive organization, in their diagrams of ideological transmission, and in their tenacious literary signification. It is well to remember that the representations of the past city were not subject to verification and could not be compared with the external realities that they professed to document, because these had already disappeared. Indeed, it was precisely the disintegration of the material past that had cleared the ground for its literary reinvention. These reinventions could be judged only as texts, validated by their internal coherence rather than their historical rigor. A dream of the past, a dream of the future — and only words and images to steer the dreaming.

With the disappearance of the tangible realities of the nineteenth century, the lettered city won the right to rework them in memory, making them conform to the ideological edifice under construction, bestowing them upon readers, and upon readers alone. The familiar groundings of people's experience had been swept away by the incessant tides of transformation, leaving them off balance, in search of a sure footing that could only be supplied by the vicarious world of the reinvented past. It was as though, detached from other points of reference, readers were absorbed altogether into the universe of signs. The persuasive permanence of that universe belies the facility with which it can be manipulated, adapted to various cultural models, and restructured to suit different meanings that can be substituted, one for another, according to the impulses of the imagination. The universe of signs offers a reassuring illusion of solidity and immobility when, in fact, it is always subtly in motion.

The cities of Latin America were thus absorbed into symbolic dioramas of themselves, then overgrown by an enchanted forest of literary signs. Among the chief contributors to the process were poets, possessed by an "impure love of cities," in the words of Cuban poet Julián del Casal. Few letrados failed to contribute somehow to the exaltation of this sacred, if impure, love: "My beloved Buenos Aires, when I see you again, there'll be no more suffering, and nothing to forget." One might think that the city of letters had crowded the city of reality totally out of the picture, but the poets of this period oscillated between the two. At least until such a time as each budding letrado became co-opted into the reigning power structure, he was available to explore the ragged margins of reality that lay outside city of letters and linger there ambiguously in what Paul Valery called a "prolonged hesitation between sound and sense," vacilating between authentic, lived experience and significations, ceremony, hierarchy, and state power. Sooner or later, most poets resolved the ambiguity by their full incorporation into the structures of power, and we can trace the transition in their poetry. We can trace it, for example, in the distance that separates the terse, ironic tremor of "Remember how you wished to be a Margarita Gautier?" from the bombast of *Canto a la Argentina*. It is still true, however, that poets are, and have always been, the least assiduous members of the lettered city, and that even after their incorporation into the orbits of power they generally appear disoriented and incongruent with their surroundings.

5

THE POLIS POLITICIZED

 The internationalist modernization of Latin America, punctuated by its own arrogant celebrations of itself in the first centenary of independence (anywhere between 1910 and 1922, depending on the country) marked a sort of rebirth for the vast region south of the Rio Grande. Somehow, the collection of fragile states separated from Spain and Portugal had become a bustling part of the world economy, had forged its modern foundations, and had become, recognizably, the Latin America of today. The major themes, problems, and challenges that animate the contemporary life of the continent were already present, in embryo, by the end of the nineteenth century. Then the politics of the twentieth century arrived, full blown, on the heels of the showy commemorations of the centenary, most strikingly in Mexico. The Mexican Revolution initiated a string of tremors throughout the region — the reflexes of socioeconomic transformations wrought by modernization, the birth struggles of a new political order to accompany those transformations. And those struggles had not yet concluded when the region was overtaken by the international economic crises of 1929 and 1973, sharpening conflicts and laying bare contradictions within Latin American societies. The twentieth century was to demonstrate how firmly the region had been incorporated into the world economy, but also how weak and dependent a position it occupied within that economy. After 1900, the distance between the center and the periphery of the international capitalist system seemed to widen, and Latin America lurched in an agitated crescendo from one crisis to another. Powerful currents of nationalism, incubated around the turn of the century, triumphed throughout the continent in the 1910s and 1920s. Then came populism, emergent in the 1930s and ascendant during much of the next half century, and finally, the catastrophic era following the international economic dislocations of 1973, the grave implications of which are only becoming evident years later.

And the lettered city? How did it weather the stormy opening of the twentieth century? Did it face renewed challenges such as those formulated by Simón Rodríguez and José Joaquín Fernández de Lizardi in an earlier period of revolutionary change? If so, what were its responses, and what influence (if there be any, worthy of consideration) did it exercise over the larger train of events? This tour, which has so far endeavored to characterize the enduring traits of the city of letters, must now relinquish the long-term perspective of social history and grapple with something more immediate and personal — family history, so to speak, and ultimately, almost biography. Here we tread a terrain inevitably fraught with judgment and prejudice, visions and confusions, realities and desires inextricably mixed, because the culturalist perception that has guided me thus far will necessarily surrender its primacy — as we enter the outskirts of the present — to another essential component of culture, politics. The final two chapters will explore the politicizing transformations of the city of letters as the vogue of "modernization" declined after the turn of the twentieth century.

Without doubt, the period of modernization brought a stronger emphasis on specialization, a more rigid division of intellectual labor — exemplified in the newly diversified plans of study at positivist universities — appropriate for societies that now confronted demands for various kinds of complex knowledge. No letrado, not even the recently professionalized journalists, could hope to master the entire sphere of letters, so all disciplines, old and new, underwent a process of more precise differentiation. Letrados became historians or sociologists or economists, and so on, while those dedicated specifically to literature became a distinct profession unto themselves: men of letters or *literatos*. As part of this process, politicians were differentiated from political scientists, but contrary to what has been extensively argued, politics did not become an entirely separate, professionalized activity. Diverse social groups and intellectual disciplines continued to take part in the political transactions of public life during the momentous opening decades of the twentieth century, participating vigorously in the political parties (some renovated, mostly new) whose debates reverberated widely in the flourishing urban journalism of the day. Peace reigned widely, and Brazil had finally abolished slavery and become a republic, but U.S. imperialism had initiated its advance in a series of events that captured the attention of all Latin America: the Spanish American War in Cuba, and Colombia's loss of Panama for the creation of an interoceanic canal by the United States, followed by frequent U.S. intervention in the Caribbean basin. In addition, the growing economic and social importance of the national state generated sharp internal debates within each country of the region, debates further enriched by a greater variety of political ideologies, including socialism, anarchism, and communism.

The literatos — it is worth repeating — were hardly absent from the intense political life of this period. Some have imagined them withdrawing from all political activity to ascend ivory towers and dedicate themselves exclusively to art. They did, of course, participate in the above-mentioned division of intellectual labor, making of their artistic vocation a profession requiring specialized, technical knowledge, and precisely for that reason they abhorred amateurs even more than their less up-to-date professional colleagues, heaping unanimous scorn on those whom Julio Herrera y Reissig called "the barber-critics," typified (for the scornful) by Remy de Gourmont's phrase as "he who understands nothing." As a result, their concentration on language and literature was more intensive than before — a circumstance highly beneficial, it must be said, to the overall development of Latin American letters — but the literatos did not withdraw from political life. To the contrary, they remained closely involved in public events, although many believed that politics were absorbing energies better spent on artistic production, something they considered fully as important to society if not more so. Nor did the twentieth century witness the extinction of the nineteenth-century model of literary statesmen like Domingo Faustino Sarmiento. Poets like Guillermo Valencia aspired to be president (of Colombia, though he failed), and so did robust novelists like Rómulo Gallegos (of Venezuela, who succeeded).

This movement of Latin American writers toward literary specialization — without abandoning a stake in public life — has not been adequately evaluated. Pedro Henríquez Ureña entitled his otherwise excellent overview of the years 1890–1920 with the less-than-apt formula, "Literatura pura," which he explained in the following terms:

> A division of labor began. Men of intellectual professions now attempted to limit themselves to their chosen tasks and abandoned politics; lawyers, as usual, did so later and to a lesser degree than did the others. The helm of state passed into the hands of those who were nothing but politicians. Nothing was gained thereby — to the contrary. And since literature was not really a profession, but rather a vocation, men of letters worked as journalists or teachers, and often, as both at once.[1]

Henríquez Ureña was probably thinking of Rubén Darío, with his all-absorbing literary passion, or of another of the modernist poets who eschewed politics, but these were the exception rather than the rule, because most literatos of the time — such as Manuel Díaz Rodríguez, José Juan Tablada, José Santos Chocano, Leopoldo Lugones, Franz Tamayo, Guillermo Valencia, even Julio Herrera y Reissig — continued to participate personally in politics or, at least, to write about it.

Writers of the day were exponents of the tenacious myth — adopted from French thought of the independence period, nourished by nineteenth-century liberalism, and steadfastly maintained thereafter by each generation of letrados — that men of letters are best suited to conduct political affairs. Far from losing its influence during late-nineteenth-century modernization, the myth became more diffuse but also more embracing. In the twentieth century, it remained robust enough for the sociologist C. Wright Mills to consider it a defining factor in Latin American intellectual life. If poets like Lugones and Valencia allowed their professional pride to convince them, contrary to all objective evidence, of their special political call-

ing, so too did the veritable phalanx of essayists who were responsible for much of the period's literary production: José Enrique Rodó,
Francisco Bulnes, Baldomero Sanín Cano, Carlos Arturo Torres,
Francisco García Calderón, Rafael Barret, José Ingenieros, Alcides
Arguedas, and many more. As for the naturalist novelists, practically
all of them were immersed in politics, a fact they demonstrated not
only in their occasional essays but also quite directly in their narrative
works.[2]

In view of Latin American traditions, it was predictable that the
literatos should retain this vision of their political vocation at a time
of rapid social transformation. As the city of letters expanded to
accompany economic growth and urbanization, it offered new fields
of activity for intellectuals who aspired to a spiritual leadership reaching beyond the partisan politics. Far from discouraging their political
participation, the social context of the early twentieth century, with
its increasing disciplinary specialization, invited Latin American intellectuals to explore fresh avenues of social influence. One can see it
in the emergence of sociology — from José María Samper to Eugenio
María de Hostos — and even more in the ideologizing function that a
majority of the period's literatos felt compelled to exercise, an ideologizing function they projected on to coming generations because
of the orientation toward youth movements characteristic of that
intellectual moment. It fell to the ideologues to provide society with
sweeping normative principles, an educational antidote to the everyday corruption of political hacks. This was the attitude evident in
Idola fori, the chief work of Carlos Arturo Torres, to which José Enrique Rodó added support in his prologue for the second edition in
1910. Indeed, the early twentieth century marked the triumphant rise
of a series of philosopher-educators whose writings were very point-
edly political, represented by Francisco García Calderón (1883–
1953) of Peru; José Vasconcelos (1881–1959) and Antonio Caso
(1883–1946), both of Mexico; Alejando Korn (1860–1936) of Argentina; and Carlos Vaz Ferreira (1872–1958) of Uruguay, among
others.

The ideologizing function assumed by writers in the period of modernization fulfilled the mission outlined by French "master thinkers" like Renan, Guyau, and Bourget. With the decline of religious belief under the withering onslaught of science, the literatos took on a role of spiritual leadership, providing a secular doctrine adapted to the circumstances and partially replacing the clergy as "keepers of souls" — in the phrase preferred by José Enrique Rodó to describe the central project of his literary generation. Physicians of the spirit, humanist priests for a new day, they stepped into the place left vacant by the decay of the established church, that formidable partner of regal power since the earliest days of colonization. But the lettered city structured its new version of spiritual power in academies, universities, and tribunals that lacked the institutional cohesiveness of the Catholic Church, and it conceived its influence as the emanation of individual talents, independent of institutional or partisan ties. Not in vain had the civil societies of Latin America begun to tread the democratizing roads of the twentieth century.

In their eagerness to replace the priesthood, the new spiritual guides adopted some of its techniques and mannerisms, such as the majestic oratorical style that lent pomp to university ceremonies.[3] They worked tenaciously to enhance the public dignity of intellectuals and even to cloak themselves in a sacred aura ("Towers of God! Poets!") as an antidote to the discordant materialism and spiritual bankruptcy of modern mass society. The intellectual's bid for a kind of sanctification gained considerable public acceptance, though that acceptance was limited, for the most part, to social sectors whose outlook had been shaped by the expansion of secular education — a portion of the lettered city already lost to the church. Paradoxically, the alienation of the more educated actually strengthened ecclesiastical influence over the unlettered masses whom the intellectuals (always more preoccupied with the formation of a new generation of the lettered elite than with the needs of the community at large) failed to address. Peasants, indigenous people, and economically marginalized urban dwellers had not benefitted — to the contrary, suffering painful reverses — because of the transformations so ardently promoted in the name of modernization, and they tended to view this self-appointed secular priesthood with skepticism and to identify the traditional Catholic clergy as their authentic defender and spiritual guide. Evidence of this attitude abounds, from the millenarian event at Canudos in the backlands of northeastern Brazil to the insurrection of the Cristeros in western Mexico.

Latin American ideologues of the period had another central role, as well, one quite specific to the region. Just as they aspired to transcend the petty corruption, personalism, and partisanism of everyday politics, they also hoped to rise above the local concerns and interests upon which everyday politics generally turned. Turn-of-the-century intellectuals sought to achieve a lofty perspective, where national destinies could be viewed in a universal context. They were the internationalists of the day — true heirs, in that respect, to the Romantic liberalism of the early nineteenth century and notable exponents of a tendency that still characterizes Latin American intellectuals in the late twentieth century. Martí's apodictic phrase defined the conviction of a whole generation: "What remains of a sleepy village in the Latin American spirit must inevitably awaken."

Immersed in the learned doctrines of Europe and the United States and — thanks to their travels and to new systems of communication — absorbed in the study of contemporary international affairs, Latin American intellectuals embraced a global ideological framework for the interpretation of regional problems. They understood only too well, through direct observation and experience, that decisions taken in the centers of international power would affect their lives powerfully, for good or ill. Thus, they advanced the integration of Latin America into the overarching intellectual discourses of the Western world, in an ideological movement complementary to the economic integration ongoing in the period of export growth. They also adapted those discourses to the social and political (even more than the spiritual) patterns of Latin American life. European racist thought found passive acceptance in the work of Francisco Bulnes, Alcides Arguedas, Rufino Blanco Fombona, and the Latin American followers of Gobineau, but it encountered stiff resistance from others, like Manuel González Prada, José Martí, and Manoel Bomfim, who were nevertheless engrossed in the intellectual concerns of Europe.

Various intellectuals of the day warned of the risk that passive Europeanization posed to Latin America's own internal traditions — traditions that, while not democratic and much less progressive, at least possessed significant legitimacy among the population at large. The most lucid thinkers strove to fashion more inclusive, syncretic cultural models that might reconcile the irresistible attractions of universalism with the maintenance of national traditions and the existing grid of social values. This undertaking seems to have come easily to poets but was considerably more difficult for novelists. As for the essayists whose work was so influential around the turn of the century, they found this task most difficult of all, and the results tended to be centrist or conservative (Torres or Rodó) more often than progressive (Martí or Bomfim).

All these writers coincided in trying to insert Latin American political discourse into the ideological debates that animated the Western world, without quite daring to attempt a total immersion. Here we see the limits of internationalization. Even the outrageously doctrinaire and derivative qualities of earlier liberalism had, by this time, undergone significant creolization (in part because of the positivist inflexions of the late nineteenth century), and that sort of unalloyed ideological imitation, irrespective of local traditions and historical experience, would not now be repeated. Early-twentieth-century anarchism, which imported its ideology intact from the industrializing Europe, constituted the principal exception to the foregoing generalization. All the other intellectual innovators of the day tried to inscribe themselves on a universal map, but in a manner reflective of the particularities of Latin American experience, without losing sight of local horizons. In 1888, José Martí, whose involvement in the belated movement for Cuban independence had resulted in his long exile in New York City, at the very heart of world modernization, formulated the cultural dilemma of internationalization in the following terms:

To the sorrow of Cubans, and of all Spanish Americans, although they inherit through study and assimilate through natural talent the hopes and ideas of one universe, the universe that moves beneath their feet is different from the one they carry in their heads. Because they come from a backward country, they have not the air, nor the roots, nor the inherent right to express an opinion concerning the questions that most absorb them. They appear ridiculous intruders if they raise their voices to address great issues facing humanity, issues of the day in countries that, unlike our own, have advanced well beyond the rudiments of civic education to achieve brilliance and power. It is as if one went crowned with lightening but shod in hobnailed boots. Truly, here is a cause for mortal woe and infinite sadness.[4]

To solve this dilemma, Martí and other Latin American intellectuals concentrated on local problems but placed them firmly within an ideological context animated by ideas, methods, and issues emanating from the centers of the modernizing world.

These international ideologies were applied now to a Latin American experience almost as pervasively urban as its overseas models. The great cities no longer stood as solitary bastions amid hostile wastes (as in the vision of the colonizers), having leveled their walls and spread confidently beyond them. Almost always political capitals, the sprawling cities had become the effective centers of control for their respective national territories and microcosms of national populations, and the problems of the city often appeared, misleadingly, to be the problems of the country as a whole. The two universes to which Martí alluded—one carried in the head while another moved beneath the feet—took objective form as two cities: the ideal city derived from well-known European prototypes, and the real city, expanding anarchically despite the efforts of those who wished to restrain and order its growth. Whether from illustrated magazines, wondrous tales told by travelers, or books setting forth urbanistic designs, visions of utopia blinded Latin American intellectuals to the social realities that surrounded them. On a spiritual level, Rubén Darío spoke of "an ideal forest that complicates the real one." Here, again, was "the cause for mortal woe," in the anguished expression of José Martí, so indicative of the tribulations of the lettered city in the modernizing era.

Let us proceed with caution: the ideal city of the time was not simply Paris — for all the Parisian-style boulevards arbitrarily imposed on Latin America's urban grids — but rather the stubborn tradition of the colonizing metropolis, conserved in the admiring spirit of its ex-colonies. The ideal was still the central city that one could dream from the periphery, thanks to the stimulation of letters and images, a dream corroborated and ratified by the centralized structure that Latin America's dominating capitals imposed on national life. Given the tenacious infiltration of present, daily experience and of the past that each of us bears secretly within, we may well suspect that Latin American understandings of the ideal city could not but differ substantially from European models, both actual and imagined. Rather than reproducing precise copies of European models, as has so often been said, the renovated cities on the western shore of the Atlantic resulted in something partly original, offspring of a desire not strictly tied to the sources of its inspiration, a desire that, in striving to *real*ize itself, must necessarily produce a muddy amalgam compounded of dreams and stubborn material realities.

Having established that the lettered city did not abandon its political vocation during the period of modernization, let us return to our turn-of-the-century benchmark, observing how the letrados' political engagement actually gained intensity when a French example activated their long-standing redemptive spirit. The immense majority of Latin American letrados continued to regard politics as a normal offshoot of the world letters, as Rodó clearly indicated in a letter to Baldomero Sanín Cano: "Perhaps you are not unaware of this inescapable fact of South American life, whereby almost all of us who live by the pen are fated to be pushed into politics. And I do not consider this entirely an evil. Everything depends on our not letting ourselves be robbed of our personalities."[5] These letrados were the versatile intellectuals of whom Latin America had so few during the Enlightenment of the eighteenth century, and, at the turn of the twentieth century, the fact of their "enlightenment" alone *fated* them to take leading roles in societies that had, as yet, barely initiated the practice of democracy.

It is worth pondering, furthermore, whether even Darío was really an exception to the rule. He did not abstain from political involvement in Nicaragua, the country of his birth, nor in the rest of the politically interconnected region of Central America. Only during his sojourns in Chile and Argentina did he refrain (by invoking his neutral status as a foreigner) from any participation in partisan politics. But that did not properly prevent him from speaking out clearly on themes of continental importance — as he maintains in his prologue to *Cantos de vida y esperanza* (1905) — nor from exercising his more general ideological function, as he says in his capital essay "Delucidaciones," which served as prologue for *El canto errante* (1907), and in which "the business of ideologues" and "the business of poets" are expressly equated.

In the study of Spanish American letters, nothing has been more broadly debated than the question of a modernist ideology. Some acute analysts, defining ideology as a coherent and explicit system, have gone so far as to deny that a modernist ideology existed at all,[6] but there can be no doubt, in my opinion, that modernist writers eagerly assumed an ideological function of some sort. This held true for the essayists and, especially, for some poets who used their carefully illuminated literary works for the exposition of doctrine: José Asunción Silva's *De sobremesa,* Manuel Díaz Rodríguez's *Sangre patricia,* and Darío's own remarkable poem, "Los cisnes." And it is hardly necessary to repeat — because it heads the list of grievances formulated against the modernists by their nationalist successors, who respected them as artists but condemned their politics — that the modernists arrogated to themselves the spiritual leadership of society, effectively abdicated by a declining church, and that they were more than willing to occupy a seat of honor on the dais of power. Many of the modernists thus collaborated in reconstructing the rigid function of the city of letters, derived directly from its colonial origins, and they could not have done so unknowingly.

The enhanced critical consciousness of the period imposed an arduous task of self-justification on the modernizing city of letters, whose renewal did not go unchallenged. No longer was it enough to produce and manipulate the discourses of administrative and judicial life at the apex of power. In order to maintain their positions as official intellectuals, those who endorsed the reigning political order—and it was the great majority, whether as public functionaries, passive supporters, or discrete fellow travelers—had to parry the attacks of intellectuals in the opposition. They did so through two principal literary and political genres, both of which were usually published in the periodical press, rather than in books, and both of which testify to the growing importance of the written word in these increasingly literate societies.

The oldest of these genres was also the most plentiful and multifarious. In modern terms, it could be called propaganda (or agitprop or *partijnost*), and it was deployed in two symmetrical branches: defense of the regime and aggression against its enemies. Political propaganda now took on a virulence previously unknown in Latin America, reaching levels of vituperation from which polemicists of the Romantic period had typically abstained. The polemicists of modernization rationalized their extreme personal invective as a theoretical advance that dissolved artificial distinctions between public and private life. The "enlightened" Peruvian intellectual Manuel González Prada made this point sententiously in his articles "Libertad de escribir" and "Propaganda y ataque," published in the late 1880s:

The criminal is just as criminal in his house as in the public square. The hyena is just as much a hyena in a cage as in the desert.

Why not harp on physical defects? The sinister cast of an eye or a stooped spinal column speaks volumes to those who understand the psychology of certain individuals. Anomalies of form usually bring moral imperfections in their train.

It is not right to hide behind the inviolability of the home, much less when, appearing to live like a damsel in the cloister, someone lives like a pig in a sty.[7]

The second political and literary genre cultivated by these defenders of the lettered city corresponded to the more prestigious field of political philosophy, which had taken the place formerly occupied by theology and metaphysics. The study of political philosophy normally went hand in hand with keen attention to history and often attempted to generate theories of the state applicable to Latin American circumstances. As one might expect, this genre had fewer practitioners, although those whom it did attract were among the most intellectually gifted writers of the day, and despite their cautious — when not frankly conservative — political horizons, their analyses were generally more lucid and comprehensive than those produced by the intellectuals of the opposition.

The names of two Mexican writers provide illustrations for these two genres — two names extracted from the teeming ranks of Porfirian intellectuals. Indeed, no country of Latin America better exemplifies the letrados' covetous approach to power than does Mexico, and this is just as one might expect in the society that, as the former Viceroyalty of New Spain, saw the creation of the first and most sustained colonial version of the lettered city. José Juan Tablada, a refined modernist poet, exemplifies the propagandistic defender of modernizing regimes. In *Tiros al blanco* (1909) and *Madero-Chantecler* (1910), Tablada "does not set forth a political doctrine nor discourse on his conservative thought," since his purpose is the direct service of immediate political interests: "to undermine the opposition to Díaz and to fawn over Huerta."[8] Justo Sierra, the most penetrating historian-sociologist of the epoch, exemplifies the political philosopher of modernization. Far superior, in this regard, to Francisco Bulnes, who is often portrayed as the quintessential Porfirian intellectual, Sierra developed his interpretation of Mexican national identity in a series of journalistic articles, eventually culminated in two extended treatments: "Mexico social y político" (1899), a long essay, and *Evolución política del pueblo mexicano* (1900–1902), a perceptive multivolume work.[9] The merits of Sierra's analysis can be attributed to the ideological coherence that he obtained by amplifying his own considerable social and political experience through the perspective of Mexico's long history.

Outside of Mexico, something similar could be said of the most vilified author and book of twentieth-century Venezuela: Laureano Vallenilla Lanz and his *Cesarismo democrático: Estudios sobre las bases sociológicas de la constitución efectiva de Venezuela* (1919).[10] Although lacking Sierra's boldness in justifying the particular government he served — that of Venezuelan dictator Juan Vicente Gómez — Vallenilla Lanz showed extraordinary perspicacity in his revision of the liberal historiography that represented the received wisdom, and he established an interpretation of *caudillismo* eventually endorsed by many modern historians. In so doing, he inscribed himself in a Latin American tradition of conservative historiography — extending from Mexico's Lucas Alamán to Colombia's Carlos Restrepo — that has been much more objective and astute than often recognized. Vallenilla Lanz based his thinking explicitly on premises of Latin American distinctiveness — or *"nuestroamericanismo,"* as advanced by José Martí — and the Venezuelan ideologue was ultimately condemned by the development, to its ultimate consequences, of one of the Cuban writer's insights: "During the years of tyranny, the republics have overcome their previous incapacity to recognize the true elements of the country, to derive from them a form of government, and to govern therewith." The same forces, inevitably corrosive of the reputations of political losers, would no doubt have besmirched Sierra's reputation, too, had it not been for Sierra's association with the university and his opportune death before the triumph of the revolution.

It is the Mexican model of the Porfiriato — which managed to survive the vicissitudes of the revolution and reconstruct itself victoriously (with much the same personnel) under Venustiano Carranza and then (beginning a pattern of periodic turnover) under Alvaro Obregón — that best allows one to detect the rationale sustaining the lettered city during these years. One can sense, in the Mexico City of Porfirio Díaz, the conjugation, with an intensity not found in other Latin American capitals, of two complementary forces: an eagerness, on the part of the letrados, to enter the charmed circles of power; and an anxiousness, on the part of the government, to attract the letrados to its service. If the general outlines of the situation are familiar, the thoroughness with which the Porfirian regime absorbed and subsidized the letrados testifies to the strength of colonial traditions that had already begun to dissolve in many countries. Somehow, this ancient ceremony of mutual attraction conserved its aura of aristocratic anointment into the era of democratization, and the magic of the written word continued to confer its indispensable prestige, not less avidly sought because publicly disputed now among Mexico's proliferating political factions.

The Mexican model depended on the weight of tradition, but also on the renewed strength of state institutions and the growth of the middle class around the turn of the twentieth century. Those who controlled the central state had far more resources at their disposal in these years of rapid economic expansion, a circumstance fortunate for educated middle sectors dependent, in some measure, on government resources — whether indirectly, in the exercise of liberal professions closely linked to the state in various ways, or directly, through public employment in education, administration, or diplomacy. Journalism, which offered intellectuals considerable autonomy in many Latin American countries and thus created some breathing room for the philosophical development of a political opposition, presents a good example of Mexico's difference in this regard. The Porfirian regime applied a systematic policy of subsidies that seemed quite successful in winning over, or at least in neutralizing, the press. As early as 1888, the opposition paper *El Hijo de Ahuizote* warned that the government was making payments — amounting to 40,000 pesos a month — to no fewer than thirty periodicals in Mexico City alone, and to most of the provincial press as well.

Dependence on the government resulted, in part, from the tiny potential readership — a real and anguishing dilemma of the writers who forged Latin American modernism. Although the creation of a reading public was among the modernists' goals, they made little headway at it, a point poignantly illustrated by the limited editions in which their works were typically published. For the most part, their readers were their own small coteries of intellectual friends and the distinguished foreign sympathizers to whom they mailed their books as gifts. Publication occurred when family and friends offered a posthumous homage to the author, when a bookseller took a personal interest in him, or, in rare cases, when a rich patron offered spontaneous munificence. The practice of literary patronage had been in decline since the time of Fernández de Lizardi, as we have seen, and the state had proved to be a poor substitute. The way of the future lay in selling one's ability in a new segment of the labor market, the writing market, where authors encountered two principle groups of buyers: politicians who needed help in composing speeches and legislation (an important item) and editors of newspapers. In either case, the identity of the writer was often erased: the speech presented in the politician's voice, the journalistic contribution published unsigned.[11]

This was the theme of Roberto Payró's wrenching play, *El triunfo de los otros,* discussed by Rodó in one of his most emotional published passages. Rodó recognized that the solution to the difficult material circumstances of Latin American writers lay in politics or journalism, which often came to the same thing: "At its better-paid levels, journalism is little more than a manifestation of politics, while at its lower-paid levels, it does not constitute an economic solution at all." Rodó's assessment of the causes of turn-of-the-century literary bohemianism led him to the pessimistic view that the earlier era of elite literary patronage had been better: "The aristocratic, individual *Maecenas* has been replaced by the plebeian collectivity. The pension that writers once received from the majordomo at the palace has been succeeded by the bookseller's trade in manuscripts." And the market for literary production in Latin American countries was so dismal that it did not even provide the dubious rewards described by Lope de Vega for seventeenth-century Spain: "the fatuous throng at least pays." Rodó concluded about the situation of writers in his own time that "the throng in question here does not pay."[12]

Rodó provided few details of problems encountered by writers entering the market for literary production because so few writers did so. (Rodó himself was a legislator who did not depend on sales of his work until after 1913.) Most writers became journalists and had to accept the political orientation and censorship of the editor of the publication that they served — something José Martí discovered as a foreign correspondent for *La Nación* of Buenos Aires. The submission to editorial authority rankled more when compounded by heavy-handed moral and political censorship, as was the case especially in Mexico. The formation of a sizable market of independent readers willing and able to buy books, already incipient in Argentina and Brazil during the first decade of the twentieth century, did not occur in Mexico for four more decades. Consequently, Mexican intellectuals remained substantially tied to the operations of the state and enjoyed less autonomy than their counterparts in other countries. Although one must approach them with caution, figures given by Francisco Bulnes illustrate the general outlines of the bitter situation in Mexico: "At the time of the restoration of the Republic, only 12 percent of all intellectuals depended on the government. In ten years, it rose to 16 percent, and before the fall of Díaz, no fewer than 70 percent got their living from government payrolls."[13]

The situation in Mexico was affected by external factors as well as internal ones. Especially noteworthy were the consequences of Martí's *"nuestroamericanismo"* in Mexican political and intellectual life. Martí advanced his ideas in various newspaper articles, particularly those written at the time of the First Pan-American Conference convened in 1889 in Washington, D.C. In the face of palpable evidence regarding the expansionist intentions of the United States, long nourished by the doctrine of Manifest Destiny, and in view of the unequal struggle likely to result from any resistance to U.S. imperialism, Martí appealed for solidarity among Latin Americans. The only defense against the U.S. expansionism lay in unity—both among Latin American nations and within each nation—against the common enemy. Like Martí's more immediate cause, the movement for Cuban independence, *nuestroamericanismo* implied a multi-class political alliance.[14] At least, so the matter was understood in Mexico, where the supporters of Díaz pointed to the universally recognized threat of the powerful neighbor to the north in silencing popular demands and resentment against the Porfirian Científicos. Thus, the dictator's agreement with U.S. railroad companies to construct the country's rail network was justified by Justo Sierra as a way both to foster national unity and to avoid irritants that might trigger latent interventionism. Craven invocation of the *yanqui* menace might not have been persuasive to Mexico's suffering poor, but it provided an acceptable explanation for the majority of Mexican intellectuals, allowing them to rationalize their acquiescence in a repressive system that — like other order-and-progress regimes elsewhere — brought some measure of economic benefit to the middle class.

Venezuela (a country lacking Mexico's long viceregal tradition) provides another example of the importance of the particular historical conjuncture in maintaining the attachment of Latin American letrados to the state during the early twentieth century. Nothing better illustrates that attachment than the parade of ministers who staffed the authoritarian government of Gen. Juan Vicente Gómez between 1908 and 1935. The dictator's ministers — charged with, among other duties, writing the six constitutions successively promulgated by Gómez — ranked among the most cultured and accomplished Venezuelans of the day. Reaching back at least to the rule of Cipriano Castro at the close of the nineteenth century, the exaggeratedly servile relationship of Venezuelan letrados to the state culminated in an almost grotesque contrast between the practically illiterate Gómez and the distinguished letrados who served him. There were, of course, not a few who resisted the dictator's blandishments, and repeated student protests (the most famous in 1928) demonstrated the existence of a tenacious, if partially submerged, current of intellectual opposition. But in the diaries written during long years of exile by Rufino Blanco Fombona, one encounters bitter comments on what he viewed as an abject surrender to Gómez on the part of the overwhelming majority of the intellectuals of the diarist's generation. In a "Nota de 1929," added to his book *La novela de dos años,*[15] Blanco Fombona attempts to discriminate between intellectuals worthy of the name and pettifoggers in the service of Gómez, who had "a certain varnish of reading and university studies" but had "an intelligence similar, or even inferior, to" that of the dictator himself. In a scathing attack on most of his contemporaries, Blanco Fombona wrote:

Under the ferocious dictatorship of Juan Bisonte [John Bison, his insulting appellative for Gómez], the "barbarocrat," the boor, the thief, the traitor, the wheeler-dealer, the butcher, the chiseler, the murderer, the executioner of students, the seller of our nationality to the *yanquis,* the destroyer of Venezuelan society by steel, fire, imprisonment, exile, plunder, poison, torture, spying, by staining the honor of men and women, monopolizing business, negating the right to hold opinions, to dissent, to breathe, even to die with dignity; under this dictatorship, the most infamous, abject, and cruel ever to dishonor America: Who have groveled at the feet of the monster? Who have prostituted themselves in the service and the adulation of the assassin, never protesting against jailings, banishments, persecutions, torments, poisonings, and larcenies? Against the surrendering of the country and its sources of wealth to foreigners and to the family of Gómez? Who have sullied themselves for a miserable pittance? Who have sung the praises of the monster? None other than the country's leading "lyric" talents: Gil Fortoul, Díaz Rodríguez, Pedro Emilio Coll, Andrés Mata, Vallenilla Lanz, César Zumeta, and many others — all, in fact, or almost all.[16]

The collaboration of intellectuals with authoritarian rule passed from grotesquery to tragedy in Mexico, as well, with the fall of Díaz and the rise of Gen. Victoriano Huerta. As the *pax porfiriana* dissolved into bloodshed, inaugurating Latin America's troubled twentieth century in the process, the peaceful tradition of bureaucratic service became obsolete, and the level of political commitment demanded of Mexico's "lyric talents" was raised from discrete partnership to the partisan belligerency exemplified by Salvador Díaz Mirón and José Juan Tablada. The treacherous execution of president Francisco Madero by reactionary forces tainted the rule of Huerta long before the triumph of the revolution brought the definitive judgment of history, but after Huerta's defeat, not a few of the intellectuals who had served him became converts to the cause of his opponent and successor, Venustiano Carranza.

By the time of Mexico's great revolutionary upheaval, a current of critical opposition thought was already clearly present, though it was still somewhat confused and inchoate and many of its exponents were recently and unevenly trained. During the ensuing decades, this current of opposition thought flowed into an idealistic, emotional, and spiritualized doctrine of social regeneration, contributed to an acerbic critique of late-nineteenth-century modernization (ignoring the opposition's own roots in that process), and launched a concerted assault on the lettered city. This assault was aimed at ousting its current occupants and at altering its ideological orientation, but not at abolishing its hierarchical function. Mexico's lettered opposition testified to the presence of an emergent middle class, the accumulative product of gradual changes wrought by modernization. Scattered across a diversity of social sectors that made the development of class consciousness more difficult, the middle class already possessed a large number of intellectual spokesmen, but it displayed a marked political preference for reform and eschewed radical breaks with the past. The uncertain exploits of the middle class were destined to loom large in the coming century, and though subsequent students of the matter have scaled back many of the sweeping assertions made in the pioneering *Materiales para el estudio de la clase media en América Latina* (1950),[17] the emergence of a middle class was already attracting the notice of Mexican politicians and intellectuals shortly after the turn of the century. The comments of Porfirio Díaz during his famous 1908 interview with journalist James Creelman testify to the dictator's own awareness of the phenomenon.

Critical thought necessarily arises within the context of what it opposes. Subtly and powerfully, reigning circumstances thus configure the opposition and impregnate it, so that critical propositions antithetical to the principles that sustain the status quo end up prolonging some of its basic orientations. Even the utopias conceived by the opposition become positive poles whose location is inescapably oriented by preexisting negative poles. Doctrines of opposition to the lettered city thus prolonged the same polarities present in the ideology against which they reacted — polarities inherent in the social context within which opposition intellectuals lived their formative years.

The social and political critiques that gained acceptance in twentieth-century Latin America had evolved during the preceding period of modernization. The economic liberalism dominant among the modernizers allowed a certain diffuseness of social development and expanded the service sector enough to permit a small flow of economic surplus to be absorbed by intellectuals involved in political dissent. Their presence was a byproduct of urbanization and, one might say, bespoke the unevenness of that process, because so many opposition intellectuals began their careers in provincial towns, where they conceived ambitions that could only be satisfied in the national capitals. The hardships of their marginal position in Buenos Aires, Rio de Janeiro, or Mexico City then steeled the resolve of these new arrivals to challenge the position of ruling elites. This is the ardent saga told so persuasively by José Vasconcelos in his *Ulises criollo*. In the twentieth century, the city of letters would be populated not only by the children of the "best" families, as had previously been the norm. Although children of privilege still figured among them, the majority of these modern letrados would be recruited from among the descendants of artisans, petty merchants, office clerks, and even, in a few extreme but significant cases, of slaves.

Paradoxically, nineteenth-century liberalism, with its philosophy of self-aggrandizing utilitarianism, figured prominently in the social genealogy of the new generation of letrados and helped account for their rise. But it did not prevent them from producing fiery indictments against the ideology that introduced material interests as primary motives of human behavior and proffered modernist hedonism as its loftiest end. As Carlos Reyles indicated in *La muerte del cisne* (1910) — opposing the arguments of his fellow Uruguayan, Rodó — the dissemination of literacy in Latin America had been the result of utilitarianism, and while the new letrados were its direct beneficiaries, they soon learned to mask the real material incentives operating in their lives and cloaked such crudities in a discourse of spirit and emotion, best systematized by Antonio Caso in Mexico: "La existencia como economía, como desinterés, y como caridad" (1919).[18] The tendency of opposition thought to disguise its own bourgeois origins in this period had been noted by Nietzsche for Europe, and it held just as true for the democratizing ideologies of twentieth-century Latin America.

A politics of interests, oriented toward immediate material improvements in people's lives, appears to have moderated the violent passions and personalisms that inevitably skew any strictly economistic analysis of nineteenth-century politics in Latin America. Of course, there are well-known limitations to any schematic economic determinism in political analysis. Still, just as Albert Hirschman has used the propositions of Montesquieu and James Stewart to argue for the case of eighteenth-century Europe,[19] "sweet commerce" tempered dominant political passions and undercut the bloody despotism of unipersonal rule in Latin America during the period of modernization. The process is evident in the liberal jurisprudence of Rui Barbosa, who promoted English legal models for his native Brazil, but evident, too, in the thinking of socialists like José Ingenieros in Argentina, and even in the formulations of anarchists like Florencio Sánchez, Uruguayan author of the polemical tract *El caudillaje criminal en Sudamérica* (1903), evocative of Sarmiento's *Facundo*. Despite the divergent sociopolitical philosophies espoused by these authors, their outlooks shared an affinity evident in retrospect, if not in their own time. Hirschman himself has cited the interpretations of two Colombian economists, Luis Eduardo Nieto Arteta and Luis Ospina Vásquez, concerning the protection that the coffee boom offered against anarchy and despotism in a country with one of the most tempestuous political histories in nineteenth-century Latin America.[20]

Abusive, personalist concentrations of power were somewhat curtailed by the expansion of commerce and industry, but such economic developments could not occur in isolation from the state, especially in the long term. The brilliant careers of Latin American captains of industry — for example, Brazil's Baron of Mauá, Argentina's Eduardo Casey, and Uruguay's Emilio Reus — often came to disastrous ends that illustrate the weakness of the national bourgeoisie, which normally had to ally itself with foreign capital and seek the protection of, or at least develop friendly links with, the power of the state. The state, in turn, had to contemporize with the regional interests of landowners and merchants, a circumstance well represented by the policies of Brazilian president Manuel Ferraz de Campos Salles, so solicitous of the interests of coffee growers in the central south of the country at the turn of the century.

Analogously, the timid advances of democracy during this period were often accompanied by the strengthening of certain authoritarian tendencies, as the circle of political power within Latin American countries widened gradually beyond the narrow limits of the landowning aristocracy to include the national bourgeoisie as well as the letrados who staffed the administrative, financial, and educational systems. Although they obviously testified to the democratic aspirations of the day, aspirations that responded less to the initiatives of the rising middle class than to the cogitations of "enlightened" intellectuals, such changes did not affect the fundamental architecture of power. Whether in the Mexico of Porfirio Díaz or the Argentina of Julio A. Roca, authoritarian governments did not decrease, but rather reinforced, what some called their "guiding influence" over the electoral process. Such governments not only continued to hold elections but increasingly emphasized their legitimating function — always under the direct control of the military, whether or not cloaked in civilian garb. Toward the end of the period, Laureano Vallenilla Lanz hit upon a description of this oscillation between contrasting tendencies in the Venezuela of Juan Vicente Gómez, calling the result "democratic caesarism." A similar idea had already occurred to Justo Sierra in Mexico, and all this well before Max Scheler and Karl Mannheim introduced the idea of a tension between the categories of "rationality" and "impulse," making dictatorship a circumstantial manifestation of the evolutionary process of democracy and a manifestation, too, of the disequilibrium between rising social classes and governing elites.[21]

Thus, the *caudillismo* that had emerged to mediate the discordant components of mid-nineteenth-century Latin American society evolved — but did not abandon its powerful grip — under the influence of "sweet commerce." Authoritarian regimes adapted themselves to the requirements of economic liberalism and cautiously admitted new social groups into the circle of power, as long as the interests of the newcomers could be conciliated with those of established ruling elites. This strategy had a variety of unintended and, perhaps, unforeseeable consequences. Of particular interest to us here is the obligatory creation of a larger group of specialists in intellectual functions. The triumph of the process of national unification — the central project of modernizing governments — had required a marked expansion of educational opportunities, had concentrated those opportunities in the cities, and had signaled the new economic importance of the lettered city in the years ahead.

6

THE CITY REVOLUTIONIZED

 Hardly had the monuments commemorating the first centenary of Latin American independence been inaugurated, hardly had the pompous foreign delegations departed, when the era of revolutions began in earnest. I share with Abelardo Villegas the idea that, if one defines revolution more as a "profound social change" than a "violent rupture with the past," then the two most significant Latin American revolutions of the twentieth century have been the Mexican Revolution initiated in 1911 and the peaceful revolution undergone by Uruguay at the same time.[1] In the same year that a triumphant Francisco Madero entered Mexico City, following the flight of Porfirio Díaz, Uruguayan president José Batlle y Ordóñez initiated his second term in office, having already defeated the armed resistance of his conservative opponents and ready now to implement his program of sweeping social and political reforms.

Although quite different from one another, both revolutions resulted in regimes that have analogues—varying in context, configuration, and degree—in later movements for sociopolitical change in twentieth-century Latin America. One could mention the early victories of Hipólito Yrigoyen in Argentina (1916) and Arturo Alessandri in Chile (1920). Then there is the "disciplined democracy" that Getúlio Vargas began to formulate for Brazil in 1930 and that carried him officially to the presidency in 1934, before his proclamation of the authoritarian Estado Novo in 1937—years in which Alfonso López was installing his "new liberalism" in Colombia and Lázaro Cárdenas was infusing new vigor into Mexico's already institutionalized revolution. One could add the successive advents of Juan Domingo Perón's "Justicialism" in Argentina (1945), Rómulo Gallegos's Acción Democrática in Venezuela (1958), Fidel Castro's armed triumph in Cuba (1959) — which raised the banner of communism in 1961 and thus helped orient Salvador Allende's Popular Unity movement in Chile (1970) — and, finally, the Sandinista National Liberation Front in Nicaragua (1980). All of these movements for political renovation drew on their own national traditions, of course, as well as on a certain historical momentum at the continental level. The purpose of the present chapter is to trace their distant origins in that momentous second birth of modern Latin America, various aspects of which have already been examined: the period of modernization surrounding the turn of the twentieth century.

In view of the foregoing panorama of successive waves of democratization — all associated with regimes redolent of *caudillismo,* when not plainly and intransigently authoritarian — we might ask whether Latin America has continued in the orbit of what has been called "democratic caesarism." By the mid-twentieth century, our scholarly interpretations of political phenomena have abandoned biological and environmental determinism and turned to the examination of more serviceable social and economic categories, and yet, as in the older literature, the figures of individual leaders remain inescapably central. Nothing better identifies the successive eruptions of new social groups (or the corresponding transformations of the political scene) than the names of their respective caudillos, and the duration of each phenomenon is not uncommonly coterminous with the leader's tenure in power.

Claudio Véliz has described "a crude and excessively assertive version of the traditional centralism" in the wake of the economic crisis of 1929, a development we have already traced back to the turn of the century, and beyond, into the period that Véliz calls the "liberal pause."[2] Other historians have found in this twentieth-century reconcentration of political power under personalist leaders not so much the resurrection of old-style *caudillismo* as a return of certain traditional political concepts still cherished by the unlettered masses who were entering the political arena for the first time. José Luis Romero has made this argument for the case of Yrigoyen and Argentina's Radical party: "The deficient political education of the new social complex impeded the realization of even its most accessible ideal, the formal perfection of democracy, because the majority sentiment brought with it a kind of 'dictatorship of the majority' that obstructed the functioning of emerging institutions precisely when it would have been easiest to establish them definitively."[3] Economists, for their part, have stressed the worsening imbalance (between center and periphery) in the distribution of international capitalism's economic surplus, especially in recent decades. Upon receiving the Third World Prize in the United Nations in 1981, economist Raúl Prebisch affirmed: "The advance of structural change in peripheral capitalism brings forth a contradiction between the process of democratization and the process of appropriation of the surplus and redistribution. There are only two options to solve this contradiction: one is to transform the system and the other is to resort to force in order to suppress democratic institutions."[4]

Historians have accustomed us to view the economic crisis of 1929 as the crucial break, the chief turning point in the twentieth-century history of Latin America, but the international oil crisis of 1973 would seem to constitute an equally significant economic break. It is now possible to see the six decades of Latin American revolutionary upheaval that began in 1910 as a coherent period characterized by enduring central issues and by debates in which the social protagonists resemble one another greatly from country to country—all conditioned by international circumstances that vary only to grow worse. The impact of the early revolutions on the lettered city thus takes on the larger implications of the period as a whole.

When, in 1924, Pedro Henríquez Ureña drew up a balance sheet of "La influencia de la revolución en la vida intelectual de México," he signaled two chief elements: nationalism and universal education. Neither was exclusive to Mexico, of course. From the time of the first centenary celebrations, they had become widespread aspirations in Latin America, sometimes explicitly attributing to Mexico the inspirational leadership that José Vasconcelos had tried so hard to establish as secretary of education for that country in the 1920s. Both elements belonged to the generational spirit of young intellectuals emerging into national life at the turn of the century, a spirit called *"ufanismo"* (later much ridiculed as hollow patriotic arrogance) in Brazil and *"novecentismo"* (in reference to the year 1900) in Spanish America, with its quintessential exposition in the manifestos of Argentina's Ricardo Rojas: *Blasón de Plata* (1909) and *La restauración nacionalista* (1910).[5]

Nationalist pride and education for everyone were causes that challenged the values — intellectual universalism and elite enrichment — characteristic of the period of modernization, but the goal was not to eliminate these values, only to complement them and create a broader social base for them. In a manner suggested by Karl Marx almost a century earlier, young intellectuals from the emerging middle class spoke with ringing tones in the name of all the excluded and dispossessed in proposing a political opening that would be most advantageous to themselves as individuals. In some ways, this was a democratic analogue of the much more elitist demands made by intellectual spokesmen years before.

According to these demands, most citizens of a nation (if not all) possessed an irrefutable right to education — a tenet that, as knowledge was assumed to confer power in society, tacitly suggested the redistribution of wealth and thus challenged the unrestricted enrichment of the elite. The suggestion remained unspoken because the young champions of this cause carefully avoided explicitly economic demands, taking instead the rhetorical high ground with expressions of lofty ideals, personal disinterest, and commitment to social justice, while accusing those in power — with a vehemence seldom equaled before or afterward — of the most scandalous greed and corruption. They maintained as well that most citizens (if not all) had rights over that vast sphere represented by the nation, doubtless more so than any foreigners, although the citizens be humble workers. In a manner reminiscent of the Creole mentality on the eve of independence, the nation figured in this discourse essentially as a provider of material benefits (the key to which lay in public office), seldom as a burden implying duties, responsibilities, or sacrifices.

However legitimate, the call for an exclusively nationalist cultural emphasis could not conceal a certain lack of intellectual rigor, as the threatened conservative doyens were quick to point out. The cultural sphere of nationalism was obviously much more accessible to the Latin American masses than the "universal" cultural knowledge prized by the "enlightened" elites in the later nineteenth century, since it was conferred automatically by place of birth and by the formative traditions of everyday life. Nor did the nationalism imply a precise ideological orientation. It served as a bulwark against both rapacious imperialism and poor immigrants, and it tended to justify an indolent resistance to any new ideas from outside the country. The rapid democratization of schooling, so superbly idealized, brought with it a predictable decline of educational standards as complex conceptual issues underwent facile popularization, and it sometimes degenerated into simple entertainment.

The populist, nationalist generation that accompanied Latin America's first twentieth-century revolutions — sometimes termed the generation of 1910 — has been obscured by the splendors of the more universalist, modernizing generations that preceded and followed it.[6] Its importance has faded, over the years, despite the fact that so many leading cultural figures emerged between 1900 and 1920: among them, Gabriela Mistral, the first Latin American winner of the Nobel Prize, representing the progress of the feminist movement in her generation; José Eustasio Rivera and Rómulo Gallegos, the first widely read regionalist narrators; and José Vasconcelos, the region's first intellectual caudillo. The experience of this generation was crucial to the subsequent transformations of the lettered city. The literary generation of the 1920s, encompassing Spanish American *vanguardismo* and Brazilian *modernismo,* displayed a renewed taste for modernism but did not relinquish the nationalizing emphasis of their predecessors. Later still, another generation of Latin American intellectuals would harken back to the writers of 1910 in the process of absorbing the revolutionary socialist doctrines associated with the Cuban Revolution.

In fact, the formula of 1910 — nationalism and education for all — translates directly, in practical terms, into "Latin American democracy." This was the banner of idealists like Simón Rodríguez in the aftermath of independence, and it echoed (hollowly, for the most part) through the political rhetoric of the rest of the nineteenth century, with some of its first artistic elaborations in the symbolist poetry of modernizing literatos at century's end. It was during the first two decades of the twentieth century, however, that the slogan began to become a practice engaging the larger national community. The catalyst for this pivotal change is not to be found in the exhortations of its intellectual architects but in the unabashed public enthusiasm for the manifestations of popular culture that now received official promotion. Wide participation in popular culture had, of course, predated official sanction of it, but had lacked a reassuring public celebration of its artistic validity, not to mention the kind of material support that now facilitated its expansion.

The cultural transformations of the period find in the sudden vogue for such things as *corridos* in Mexico and *tangos* in Argentina a better emblem than in the frequently mentioned lectures on the transformations of Western thought at the Ateneo de la Juventud Mexicana (1909) or in Ricardo Rojas's literary revalorization of Argentine provincial life. The living popular culture of the moment was not the conservative, declining folk heritage of the countryside that urban intellectuals admired for its picturesque local color. It was the vital, vulgar culture of the urban masses, who drew on rural folk traditions as the natural matrix of their own creativity but did so without a nostalgic urge to conserve. The exuberant popular culture of Latin America's great cities testified instead to the present — to the experience of rapid urbanization and to the emergence of a working class as a major historical protagonist. Nothing better illustrates this process than does the career of the tango, which passed from its birthplace in brothels and poor neighborhoods to the fashionable salons of the middle class as Buenos Aires and Montevideo swelled explosively with rural migrants and immigrants from overseas during the first twenty years of the century. It took considerably longer for the middle class to embrace urban popular culture in Mexico, where attitudes like those revealed by even so subtle an intellectual observer as Antonio Caso — who spoke of "hopelessly ignorant common people" — impeded the valorization of their cultural dynamism.[7]

Politically, the dissenting letrados of the period no longer formulated the transformations they desired in closed and often secret organizations like the masonic lodges of the independence period. They had come to view mass-based party organizations, quite unlike the elite alignments of the nineteenth century, as the essential vehicles of political change. It is interesting to observe, at the risk of digressing slightly, that not until well after mid-century would Latin American intellectuals resort again to a pattern of secret organization reminiscent of the lodges, justifying their abandonment of party politics in theoretical terms provided by Régis Debray's *Revolution in the Revolution* (1962). Debray interpreted the experience of the victorious Cuban Revolution and proposed the creation of insurgent nuclei called *focos* to stimulate the spread of revolutionary activity. It ought to be added, as well, that the late-twentieth-century reversion to a strategy of secret vanguard organizations (which began to acquire a mythic aura in Franqui's slender book *Los doce*) failed to do justice to a revolutionary movement that had, by that time, touched broad sectors of the population.

However committed to the idea of mass-based party politics, the intellectuals of the first period of democratic opening remained firmly within the parameters of the Latin American political tradition. The sole aim of their political action was taking over the government, and they conceived of no manner of generating social change apart from control of the central state, now more powerful than ever before. They distinguished their objectives from those of earlier opposition movements by specifying their intent to use the power of the state to democratize and not, as in the past, to serve the narrow interests of one elite faction or another. Ultimately, in this way of thinking, the progress of democratization would contribute to reducing ubiquitous governmental power. The generosity of their idealism does not conceal its flaws: an inability to imagine forms of democratization less dependent on the state and a failure to reflect on the capacity of institutionalized power to reproduce itself in ever more rigid and authoritarian forms. These potential hazards made themselves felt quickly indeed, if one credits the testimony of intellectuals like José Vasconcelos who, in his *Memorias,* shows how each successive group taking control of the Mexican state after 1910 concentrated power further and rode more roughshod over those who did not belong to the inner circle. There was, perhaps, truth in Alberto Zum Felde's skeptical observation that "the difference between 'enlightened' and 'barbaric' dictatorships lay mostly in how they were regarded by intellectual minorities."[8]

If "democratic caesarism" seems less than satisfactory as a description of politics in a period that insistently termed itself nationalist, perhaps "democratic authoritarianism" will do. Either formula indicates that a democratic outlook substituted for the aristocratic one of enlightened despotisms (the best example of which in Latin America was the reign of Pedro II in Brazil). But both display an obvious contradiction, since caesarism and authoritarianism are better adapted to a hierarchical society than to a democratic one, in which cultural values are not handed down from a ruling elite but forged in the free interplay of social forces and merely implemented by the rulers. The contradiction was expressed as well in the tenacious aristocratic tendencies of the lettered city, which aspired to carry on a tradition of cultural leadership parallel to the political leadership of the new caudillos. Nevertheless, a clear cultural change occurred as Latin America's twentieth-century cycle of revolutions unleashed truly transformative forces in successive waves, ever widening the circle of political participation with the inclusion of new social groups, a development well illustrated by the evolution of art and letters during the first half of the century. The activities of members of the city of letters contributed importantly to the process of cultural change, because crusading letrados made partisan appeals to the poor and recently educated in an effort to further the cause of populist nationalism and, as a result, encouraged the political expression of ideas, values, and sensibilities rooted in the collective experience of the popular classes.

Hence the singularities of the partisan politics that arose in Latin

America around the turn of the century, riveting the attention of political thinkers and actors on new democratic parties. These parties were endowed with an organic structure and mobilized a solid participatory base (reaching into many sectors of the population) around a coherent program of ideas. Although they continued to hang their hopes of social renovation on the seizure of political power—whether in elections or revolutions—the road to victory in either case seemed to lie in the democratic politicization of the party's mass base. In some countries, that politicization would be urgent, tempestuous, and driven by events; in others, where the institutions of political representation were already more consolidated and the perspective of eventual triumph more certain, it would advance more patiently. The salient example of the first pattern is the party that Francisco Madero set in motion on the eve of the Mexican presidential election of 1910, a party that did not come fully—and then, only precariously—into being until after the revolutionary victory, in response to the series of government initiatives that culminated in the formation of the country's Partido Revolucionario Institucional (PRI). The second pattern is perhaps best exemplified by the democratizing renovations enacted by José Batlle y Ordóñez within Uruguay's veteran Colorado party in preparation for the elections that carried him to power in 1903 and again in 1911. Similarly, Argentina's Unión Cívica Radical saw its many years of dedicated organizing finally crowned by the election of Hipólito Yrigoyen in 1916.

One could cite many other Latin American examples of the contrasting roads inaugurated by Madero and Batlle, respectively. For example, precisely the same dichotomy could be applied to the Partido Revolucionario Cubano, forged in 1892 by José Martí in preparation for an invasion of the island three years later, and, on the other hand, the Partido Republicano of Brazil, that began its gradual proselytization under the leadership of Quintino Bocaiuva in 1870 and achieved the overthrow of the monarchy only after eighteen years of patient organization. Some parties vacillated between the two paradigms. The frustrating experience of Peru's Unión Nacional (established in 1891) throws light both on the character of its founder,

Manuel González Prada (who abandoned the project and embarked for France after only a few months), and on the social forces in conflict in that sorely divided Andean nation, where democratization began to gain headway only in the 1920s.

The new mass-based parties built on the critique that opposition letrados had directed in preceding years at the insufficiencies and falsehoods of "politics as usual." The writings of Manuel González Prada offer some particularly virulent examples. The Peruvian literato inveighed, in various essays, against parties (calling them "electioneering clubs or mercantile associations"), against politicians ("a syndicate of sickly ambitions"), against politics ("treachery, hypocrisy, bad faith — corruption in white gloves"), and against leaders in general ("agents of high finance, shrewd bumpkins who have turned a profit in politics, impulsive soldiers who regard the presidency of the republic as the highest rank in a military career").[9] González Prada nevertheless resisted the idea of a strict, specific party platform and instead espoused general formulas that often seem fatally vague: "to evolve in the direction of widest individual liberty, preferring social reforms to political transformations." On the other hand, he specified categorically that the members of a party ought to rally around elevated ideals and moral principles. In his "Declaración de principios" (1891) he says that "it is especially important to unite men with the bond of ideas,"[10] and in his public lecture "Los partidos y la unión nacional" (1898), he defends the partisan principle of refusal to compromise: "In only one way — by being intransigent and irreconcilable — will we attract the sympathy of the crowd and find an echo in its soul. Why have our political parties failed in the past? Because of the lack of real dividing lines, because of the mutual infiltration of one side by the other."[11]

The vision of party as an ideological bulwark — that gave no quarter to its adversaries and never compromised on matters of doctrine — was a defining feature of the new political forces, at least in their period of ascendance. For the Río de la Plata, this penchant for ideological purity can be observed full blown in the democratizing parties of Yrigoyen and Batlle, which took on an exclusivism highly irritating to the older parties and especially unbearable to political independents, who attributed it to the personal despotism of the two caudillos. In Uruguay, for example, "Batllismo" tolerated the presence of a minority opposition within the government, but policies were set by the majority party in strict accordance with its guiding philosophy. The political intervention of intellectuals was limited to their participation in the ranks of one party or another, as they became, first and foremost, *correligionarios*—adherents of a partisan creed. Among the first to express their resentment were the great cultural figures of the turn-of-the-century modernization period, such as José Enrique Rodó, whose relations with Batlle were notably strained. When Batlle announced his second presidential candidacy in 1910, Rodó endorsed it along with most other members of "the conservative classes for whom the prestige of administrative order is always what most adorns the image of a public man, along with the country's working-class elements who had acquired a collective consciousness for the first time during the government of Batlle."[12] By a year later, however, Rodó had distanced himself from Batlle and joined the opposition, vowing to combat "the disastrous politics of closed factions, the deliberate exclusion from the government of the country's most representative intellectual and moral forces, the overwhelming personalism of presidential authority, smothering all autonomies and effectively suppressing all divisions of power."[13]

The same ideological purism that excluded some letrados from power provided privileged access to others, in a pattern that recurred thereafter in the Brazil of Getúlio Vargas, the Argentina of Juan Perón, and even the Cuba of Fidel Castro. Batlle was accompanied in his rise by a group of new intellectuals, many of them little-known members of Montevideo's literary bohemia, who now began to develop an active political militancy. Some, like Leoncio Lasso de la Vega and Angel Falco, were anarchists who struggled to garner the support of their own organizations for the Batllista cause.[14] Others (José Pedro Bellan, Enrique Casaravilla Lemos, Alberto Zum Felde) were members of the recently educated middle class. Perhaps the best example of this new generation of Batllista intellectuals, however, was the writer-turned-politician Domingo Arena. Thus, the predictable result of the more ideologically disciplined party lines was not only a generational turnover in the Uruguayan city of letters and a greater diversity of social origins among its membership, but also, and above all, closer relations with the government and stronger identification with its policies and initiatives.

For another perspective on the changing character of the city of letters, let us look more closely at the letrados' commitment to the democratic base of the new parties that were founded around the turn of the century and triumphed during its initial decades. These letrados were not yet "organic intellectuals," in the sense intended by Antonio Gramsci, for such did not begin to figure significantly in left organizations until the 1940s. Yet a powerful commitment to the democratic base is evident in José Martí's tenacious efforts to create a Partido Revolucionario Cubano, a project that had long germinated in his mind before culminating in the formal party organization of 1892. Eight years previously, Martí had broken with insurgent general Máximo Gómez precisely because of the authoritarian structure that the military leaders had given to the Cuban independence movement. "One does not found a country, General," wrote Martí on that occasion, "the way one commands a military camp."[15] The democratic orientation of the movement was crucial for Martí, as he made clear in his 1887 proposal to General Juan Fernández Ruz, reaffirming both the need for ideological purity (consequently rejecting an alliance with those who would free Cuba from Spain in order to annex it to the United States) and the need for a revolutionary solution with "well-known democratic ends."[16] The democratic character of the revolutionary "clubs" that were eventually organized in New York, Cayo Hueso, and Tampa is doubly interesting since their aim was to organize an invasion of Cuba. Despite their military purpose, these clubs guaranteed the free expression of their members' opinions and decided most matters in an egalitarian manner hedged only by the limited attributes of their annually elected officers. In addition, Martí's movement absorbed previously existing clubs of Cuban émigrés that brought their own democratic traditions into the Partido Revolucionario Cubano.[17]

In the Río de la Plata, the democratizing movements of Yrigoyen and Batlle operated under more favorable conditions and with wider popular participation that combined to give their efforts larger success and greater durability. Henceforth, endowed with a solid political integration and a reliable ideological framework, the emergent middle sectors of Argentina and Uruguay would maintain their important role in national life. To the extent that similar developments were taking place during the early decades of the twentieth century throughout Latin America, we can account for the third defining feature of the political movements that placed their stamp upon the period: nationalism.

The spirit of national solidarity had diverse origins. For the case of Argentina, Arturo Andrés Roig has emphasized Yrigoyen's interest in the German philosopher Karl Krause, and it is suggestive that Martí and Batlle also received the influence of Krause via readings of Spanish Krausists such as Francisco Giner.[18] The circumstance shows, once again, the original adaptation that Latin Americans invariably make of European intellectual currents. Sometimes, as in the case of Krausism, the Latin American adaptations take on substantially greater importance than the original currents possessed in their counties of origin. Max Nordau waxed indignant on what he viewed as the exaggerated influence of Krausism in Spain and Latin America: "In Germany, I am sure that not even professors of metaphysics know of [Krause] . . . yet the Spanish study him, gloss him, and admire him."[19] Krausism encouraged the members of a party to envision themselves as spiritual regenerators, caretakers of the national essence, crusaders on a redemptive mission — an attitude that powerfully reinforced the cultural ties that bound them together. According to Abelardo Villegas:

The radicalism and the essentialism of his party implied, for Yrigoyen, a complete identification of his movement with the good of the *Patria*. . . . The result was a kind of sanctification, as the mystique of the party became a "civic religion"; Yrigoyen became an "apostle"; the party members, his "*correligionarios*"; and defection, apostasy. Not in vain did Yrigoyen himself equate Krausist solidarity with Christian solidarity. Therefore, it was logical that having (theoretically) rejected the system of partisan factions, for some Yrigoyenists the citizens of Argentina could be divided only into the pure, like themselves, and their impure adversaries.[20]

An accent on ideological program, on democratic organization, and on national solidarity thus defined the new partisanism of the early twentieth century, but much remained the same. The caudillo-style charisma of certain leaders continued to be a marked characteristic of political life, the thirst for personal power found new opportunities as the state expanded its attributes and its radius of action, and partisan exclusivism became, if anything, more intense. A pervasive aura of civic religion impregnated the new mass-based parties. And, despite the persuasive arguments of a number of historians to the effect that a certain class orientation was a consequence — rather than an antecedent — of the new partisanism, these movements could not have been created independently of the worldview of the emergent social classes. One can point, for corroboration, to the transformation of cultural horizons occurring during this period across Latin America. It was particularly strong in the Río de la Plata, with its journalistic celebrations of urban popular culture (in the magazines *Caras y caretas* or *Fray Mocho,* for instance) and with its popular nativist drama, newly respectable (Juan José Podestá on the stage of the Apollo Theater) and able to reach even the illiterate. But good examples are not lacking for Mexico, as well, with its proliferating penny press and the broadsides that made the reputation of Antonio Vanegas Arroyo — media vigorous enough to support the development of an entire school of popular illustrators, from Manuel Manilla to José Guadalupe Posada.[21]

Still, important contrasts differentiate the Mexican experience of revolutionary rupture from the experience of gradual evolution in the Río de la Plata. Mexico's tradition of elitism created such marked distinctions between variants of popular and high culture that James D. Cockcroft felt forced to use a hierarchical organization in his discussion of revolutionary intellectuals.[22] In the Río de la Plata, on the other hand, the lettered city showed less rigidity and a greater sense of commonality uniting sons of the nineteenth-century oligarchy (like Lucio V. Mansilla and Eduardo Wilde) with the obscure, upwardly mobile sons of the provincial or capitaline middle classes. The relative autonomy of Argentine or Uruguayan intellectuals, along with other factors—among them, their capacity to detect the prevailing direction of social change and the bourgeois rationality of their analyses, reinforced by the shared experience of urban residence and the constant intellectual exchange facilitated thereby—all combined to temper and inform their reaction to demands advanced by working-class and white-collar groups.[23]

Wherever these changes occurred, the new generation of intellectuals—with their confident vision of a future society inspired by modern European models but adapted to local conditions—had set about using their political influence to orient the rest of society. As a result, the lettered city had itself been transformed, within a relatively short lapse of time, from a handful of elite letrados designing government policies in their own image, into a socially more heterogeneous group that retained a vision of itself as a cultural aristocracy but incorporated powerful democratizing cross-currents. During this transitional phase—when the democratic opening had already begun but the triumph of mass-based political parties was not yet imminent—some intellectuals attempted a kind of political action not aimed directly at taking control of the government. They could do so because of the emergence of a mass reading public at the same time. Universal public education, long a cherished goal, had now become a real focus of government policy, and economic growth created previously undreamed of resources for intellectual action independent of state tutelage. The result was the development of intellectual activities not only independent of the state but actually in opposition to it. This generation of opposition letrados deserves special attention because of the precedents they set. They designed the first independent road to power traveled by Latin American intellectuals, some of whom still attempt to travel that same road in the present day.

In spite of the growing size of the lettered city at the turn of the twentieth century, the intellectuals who composed it were still a relatively compact group. In that patrician politicians continued to function as poets, historians, or jurists, there was more connection between the city's political and humanistic sectors than would be imaginable today, and to the degree that journalists and writers participated in mobilizing the working class, there were more real links between letrados and labor organizations at the turn of the century than in the 1930s (when such links became so central to left ideology). The changing shape of the urban environment — as commercial, industrial, and residential spaces became increasingly segregated from each other — helped maintain the spatial focus of the lettered city during this transitional period. As so-called "decent" society began its exodus toward new residential districts far from the center of town and recent immigrants continued to swell poor neighborhoods, also on the periphery of the city proper, the old downtown area preserved and even intensified its public function. "It continued to be the administrative and commercial center in almost all cities," notes José Luis Romero, "but only in a few — Rio de Janeiro and Buenos Aires especially — did it modernize architecturally and maintain its prestige."[24] The area around the central plaza still brought together public and private administration, finance, commerce, and entertainment, so that people engaged in one activity rubbed elbows with those involved in another. Whether for shopping, employment, or diversion, "to go downtown" remained the periodic obligation of those who lived far from the center, in residential neighborhoods that lacked business districts of their own.

Take out a map of a major Latin American city at the beginning of the twentieth century and try to locate the following: the houses inhabited by writers (usually boarding houses in the case of provincial letrados who had come to the national capital for study or employment); the offices of the newspapers (where such writers worked as reporters or at least contributed occasional stories); the government agencies (the post and telegraph office, archives, libraries, ministries, and so on) that constituted their chief source of employment; the universities where they studied a liberal profession (abandoned soon after graduation); the lecture and concert halls (locales of their learned disputations); the cafés where they seemed to spend most of the day (writing, discussing literature, or seeking financial support); the theaters that they attended (to write a review, peddle a script, or pursue an actress); the law offices (where they functioned as clerks or merely chatted about art); the party headquarters (where they practiced their oratory, the most celebrated skill of the day and that which most defined an intellectual); the brothels (that they attended assiduously until the day they were married); the churches (where at least some repented of their sins); and, finally, the stores selling fine furnishings and objets d'art (imported from Barcelona or Paris). Together, these locations signal the outlines of the old city center, a quadrilateral of about ten blocks on each side, scene of public business and sociability, the place where novelists of the day inevitably plotted the "chance" meetings of their characters.

This is the relative handful of intellectuals (perhaps less than a hundred in Buenos Aires or Rio de Janeiro when each of those cities was already reaching toward a million inhabitants) who attended the voracious demands of the reading and theater-going public at the turn of the century. They had little sense, initially, of what popular proclivities would be when no longer restricted by the "enlightened" tastes of letrados such as themselves, and in their consternation they tended to echo the condemnations of "mass culture" already formulated by English and French critics. Their first encounter with this challenging new public was in the theater, where audiences attending light comedy (in Rio de Janeiro) or swashbuckling gauchesque melodramas (in Buenos Aires) were not necessarily even literate. Let us give the floor to a few eye witnesses. In his *Recuerdos literarios,* Martín García Merou evokes the struggle of Argentine authors to found a national theater in the 1870s, using sophisticated themes that uniformly emptied auditoriums altogether after an opening night populated mostly by family and personal friends:

Need I say that all our beautiful dreams, like those of the milk maid in the fable, went up in smoke? Ah, we all know it only too well! A decade has passed, and the insoluble problem of the national theater has been resolved by a clown [here referring to Juan José Podestá's successful "*criollo* clown," Pepino el 88] with an actor's instincts and temperament, who has transformed a tasteless circus pantomime into a series of scenes dramatically recounting the life of a legendary bandit. In a supremely ironic comment on intelligence and art, [the adventures of the bandit] *Juan Moreira* have achieved what Coronado's *La rosa blanca* or *Luz de la luna y luz de incendio* could not do.[25]

For an amusing reversal, let us next lend an ear to Artur Azevedo, panned by sophisticated Brazilian critics for his vulgar popularity. Azevedo left a pleasant autobiographical account of his arrival in Rio de Janeiro (from distinctly provincial origins in São Luís de Maranhão) at the age of 18. Here he recounts the consequences of his repeated failures in writing for the serious stage: "In sum, every time that I tried to do serious theater, I was repaid only with censures, nicknames, and injustices, with precious little pay; while, trying my hand at light comedy, I never lacked for praise, parties, applause, and remuneration. Excuse me for mentioning this last, glorious item but, the devil if it's not essential for a breadwinner who lives by the pen."[26]

From about 1890 on, the theater of most of Latin America's capital cities opted for the same vulgar popularity condemned by the critics of Azevedo (and many others, whether conservative, like García Merou, or progressive, like Florencio Sánchez) until, in the 1920s the stage was devoured by the cinema (which adapted from it a number of original expressive forms). The rise of the popular theater between 1890 and 1920 was paralleled precisely by the vigorous commercialization of popular music, especially as dances for worldly urban settings. Across Latin America, composers stylized and polished musical ideas of rural, folk origin, and poets added lyrics — some memorable, all agreeable to the sensibilities of the rising middle classes. Hence the wide vogue, at this time, of popular musical forms like *jarabes, corridos, joropos, danzones, habaneras, boleros, guarachas, sambas, batucadas, guaguancós, plenas, golpes, merengues, cumbias, tangos, choros,* and so on. Even the composers of erudite music (repeating one of the most characteristic maneuvers of the Latin American *intelligentsia*), upon noticing the musical nationalism of Europe, really listened, at last, to the rhythms that they had heard around them since infancy. Gerard Béhague aptly summarizes these developments: "A definable national music style appeared only in the last decades of the century, under the influence of similar trends in Europe and the emergence of musical genres with folk and popular characteristics which could constitute an obvious source of national identity."[27]

European models influenced cultural production for the eyes, as well as the ears, of the new mass public. The sort of narrative previously appearing by daily installments to capture the distracted attention of newspaper readers was now published separately in the form of dime novels. During the 1880s, the newspaper *La Patria Argentina* stayed in business partly thanks to stirring tales by Eduardo Gutiérrez, whose *Juan Moreira*, first appearing in 1879–80, helped establish the stock image of the good gaucho gone wrong. The novels of Gutiérrez eventually merited sumptuous editions by the Spanish publishing house Maucci, and Spanish publishers also distributed the complete works of one of the most successful Latin American novelists, José María Vargas Vila (1860–1933) of Colombia. Known for his poetic sensualism and ridiculed by the defenders of high culture as a purveyor of "literature for maids," Vargas Vila achieved early success with his *Flor de fango* (1895) and went on to produce no fewer than forty titles, making him one of the foremost professional writers of the day. His spicy novels attracted middle-class women, as well as servants, but they were hidden from impressionable daughters, who instead received more straight-laced and educational reading material, like the books of Hugo Wast (a pen name, his real one being Gustavo Martínez Zubiría) of Argentina. Despite their conservatism, Wast's numerous novels — from *Flor de durazno* (1911) to *Lo que Dios ha unido* (1945) — sold enough to provide him with 20,000 pesos in annual royalties by the early 1920s.

The years before 1920 saw the creation of Latin American publishing houses that were to provide the region's intellectuals with direct access to the reading public and some measure of independence from the state. Maucci began to function in Mexico City, Librería de H. Garnier appeared in Rio de Janeiro, and Roberto Payró helped to establish the Biblioteca de *La Nación* in Buenos Aires. (It was not uncommon for newspapers to publish books on the side, and Payró was a well-known journalist at *La Nación*.) These publishers measured their runs in the French manner, by thousands of copies, though some smaller publishers seldom surpassed runs of five hundred, and repeated printings were frequent. In a catalogue put out by H. Garnier around 1910, one observes that *As religões do Rio* had been through seven printings in six years. Of course, this was a work of wide appeal by João do Rio, one of the city's best-known journalists and a leading member of its "café society."[28] A pile of magazines, other periodical publications, and popular literary collections (stimulated by the takeoff of the novel) enjoyed intense, if ephemeral, activity at this time. By the 1920s, one could even speak of a "boom" (which modestly declined, however, to present itself through such marketing terminology). At last, the aspiration of Latin American authors—to speak to their public unconstrained, without depending on the state for a livelihood or for the means of publication—seemed to be at hand. The new situation transformed the city of letters in many ways, three of which merit extended discussion: the incorporation of social doctrine, the rise of the self-educated, and professionalism.

The incorporation of social doctrine. Of all the ideologies that influenced the city of letters in the twentieth century, none was more fertile than the early introduction of anarchist thought. The ground had been prepared by other versions of utopianism, such as that espoused in the *Cartilla socialista* of Plotino Rhodakanaty, published in 1861 when he was recently disembarked in Mexico. Latin American anarchism, like Latin American liberalism, was highly sensitive to European models, but after 1900 (when it had to compete with other social doctrines like socialism and, eventually, communism) it had sunk roots and no longer seemed such an exotic import. Anarchists opposed the idea of partisan politics—a circumstance that increased their importance to the development of a current of critical thought at the margins of state power — but they shared the educational goals of the new mass-based parties. Their vision of education was holistic — including family life, labor relations, social hygiene, anticlericalism, and the rights of women (of which the anarchists were pioneering exponents) — and it focused particularly on the most needy, the proletariat. The proselytizing of this social doctrine produced the Centros de Estudios Sociales and the first open universities, following the example of the famous Escuela Moderna, established in Spain by Francisco Ferrer, who was viewed in the Spanish-speaking world as the authority on truly free education. Although the new radical social doctrines developed originally within the ranks of labor organizations with largely foreign membership, their rapid nationalization can be traced in documents such as those collected for the Brazilian case by Edgard Carone. In 1896, the Centro Socialista announced the books available in its library, almost all of them in French, but in 1919, the Communist Party already offered translations of Kropotkin, Grave, Marx, Darwin, and Gorki.[29] The nationalization of the new social doctrines took place even more rapidly in Mexico, where anarchists were active in the popular insurrection, though — to judge, a least, by the pages of Flores Magón's *Regeneración* or by the dissidence voiced at the founding of the Casa del Obrero Mundial — their objectives differed considerably from those of allied groups. In the books of Hart, García, and Cockcroft, one can gauge the acceptance that anarchist and socialist currents found among intellectuals in the lower strata of society — young men of limited means who alternated between study and manual labor and who frequently dropped out of the universities dissatisfied.[30]

The rise of the self-educated. Whether for economic reasons or intellectual ones, the universities were losing the monopoly that they had enjoyed throughout the nineteenth century as the only avenue to letrado status, and self-taught men of letters gained a dignity previously unknown. Even during the apogee of positivism and modernization at the close of that century, the universities had remained the formative centers for future professionals and public officials, imparting a clear hierarchical order to the lettered city. Partly under the influence of anarchism, there emerged in the early twentieth century a group of intellectuals, usually from a lower social class, who could not afford or did not desire a university education. The texts of the self-taught intellectuals were to be found in the free market of books and magazines, and their seminars were conversations in cafés and other informal meeting places. The confused and tumultuous process of democratization was creating a new type of letrado who, lacking contact with the most esteemed instrument of formal education, necessarily developed a less disciplined and systematic, but also more liberated, intellectual vision. It was within the ranks of professional writers that the self-educated congregated, because their access to other professions was being restricted, during these same years, by new governmental dispositions that limited the exercise of most professions to the holders of specific degrees.

In Mexico, the self-taught composed the most advanced rebel group in Cockcroft's classification of prerevolutionary intellectuals, one end of a spectrum defined, at its other extreme, by the young men gathered in the Ateneo de la Juventud, whose strong orientation to the university revealed the persistence of traditional elitism. The rise of the self-educated was not particularly linked to Mexico's revolutionary commotion, however, as is demonstrated by their even more robust presence in other parts of Latin America where democratization took a less turbulent course. The situation in Uruguay, for example, is thus described by Alberto Zum Felde, himself a member of the group of intellectuals who worked for the reelection of José Batlle y Ordóñez to a second term in 1911:

The "café intellectual," who first appeared around 1900, was an entirely new phenomenon on the Uruguayan scene. Until that time, the university intellectual had been the only sort. All writers, lecturers, and publicists in the country were products of university classrooms, where they had pursued disciplinary studies and finished with academic degrees. The "doctor of laws" was the Uruguayan intellectual par excellence, whether in politics or letters. The generation of the Ateneo was a generation of *doctores*. But after the turn of the century, the *doctor* became only the political sort of intellectual, and from then on, the most notable writers were self-educated, with few university courses to their credit, or none at all.[31]

The advent of the professional writer. Far from being unrealistic dreamers, these self-taught intellectuals were quite attentive to the demands and opportunities of their profession. They perceived the rapid development of a mass reading public. According to Horacio Quiroga (1878–1937), if the professionalization of the writer's craft was still in the "stone age" during the 1890s, it moved into the "iron age" after 1900 amid a veritable explosion of periodicals discussing public affairs. In the proliferation of magazines and newspapers, aspiring writers took the measure of the literary market, with "its fluctuations, its bitter disappointments, and its unexpected pleasures" (Quiroga's words again), and they took special pride in the relative independence assured them by that market's new vigor.[32] They did not earn enough to live exclusively from their writing, and they still had to please the editors of the newspapers and magazines, of course, but they were at least free of the tyranny of governmental patronage, and that compensated for trials imposed by their rocky incorporation into the logic of market capitalism, a logic which they had only recently accepted. Manuel Gálvez (1882–1962), who made his debut in 1903 with a magazine called *Ideas* and eventually sold 40,000 copies of his novels in Buenos Aires alone, cited a commercial orientation as a distinguishing characteristic of his literary generation:

The professional writer, as a type, appeared in Argentina with my generation. By professional, I do not mean a writer who lives exclusively from literature, because that phenomenon is almost unknown here, except among the authors of plays, but rather the man who spends his time principally on literary work, who publishes books with regularity, and who, though he many not try to live on his earnings as a writer or journalist, tries at least to make ends meet with them.[33]

Professionalism, like the cultivation of a reading public upon which professional status depended, had been an idealized aspiration for Latin American writers throughout the nineteenth century, and like the advent of a reading public, the professionalization of the writer's craft proved a mixed blessing when it finally did occur. The demands of professionalism wrecked the literary ambitions of many, but the struggle to succeed in the marketplace became the crucible in which true vocations were forged. An example of the commercial tug-of-war between author and editor—negotiating the prices and conditions of literary commodities—can be observed in the correspondence between Horacio Quiroga and Luis Pardo, who was in charge of the magazines *Caras y caretas* and *Fray Mocho*.[34] Quiroga later described the editorial demands of his friend Pardo:

His demands for brevity in stories were exceptionally severe. A story could not be longer than one page, including the space for the accompanying illustration. To develop believable characters, to place them in a setting, then to draw readers out of their habitual indifference, interest them, involve them, and shake them up— all that the writer had was one single, narrow page. Better yet: 1,256 words.[35]

Budding professional writers found that the demands of the literary marketplace determined not only the length of their compositions, but also their lexicon, their poetic rhythms, and their artistic resources. Nimbly simplified, these were to be put at the service of nationalist messages, inventories of the natural and social environment, and applications of historical understandings to present concerns, the whole to be liberally sprinkled with the moral didacticism characteristic of the period. The requirements of the marketplace specified that literary products had to be easily intelligible to recently educated members of the middle and lower-middle classes. Manipulative sentimentalism was to be cultivated rather than avoided, and historical settings were to be presented in typical operations of nationalist (re)connaissance. Of Baldomero Sanín Cano in Argentina, of Carlos Sabat Ercasty in Uruguay, or of Sabat Ercasty's brilliant Chilean disciple, Pablo Neruda, one could repeat what a critic has written of their counterpart in Mexico: "ordinary Mexicans discovered and contemplated themselves in the poetry of [Ramón] López Velarde."[36]

In other ways, however, the experience of Mexican writers during the years of revolution was quite different from that undergone by their colleagues in the southern hemisphere, which made it more typical of the larger twentieth-century experience. The period of modernization had brought only elusive signs of democratization to Mexico, leaving the country's old elitism intact and vigorous. As discussed previously, Mexico's letrados continued to cultivate their distance from popular culture, and the concomitant exclusivism led them to place strict limits on access to the city of letters. Neither in the countries of the southern cone nor in Brazil does one find evidence, in this period, of the vision that led Mexican intellectuals to create their Ateneo de la Juventud in 1909. If Mexican intellectuals clearly shared the same concern for the expansion of educational opportunities that motivated their southern counterparts, they evinced even greater interest in the creation of advanced degree programs. A similar desire for further development of the institutions of higher education was expressed only in Peru and Colombia — not coincidentally, the two other centers where viceregal power had led to the full flowering of the lettered city during the colonial period.

Mexican intellectuals also faced a different sort of social challenge in the early twentieth century. Instead of an electoral offensive mounted largely by the middle class, they confronted military caudillos, often of humble origins and frequently hailing from rural areas subject to modernizing influences from the United States. The triumphant insurgents from the border state of Sonora had felt those influences abundantly and seemed to derive part of their surprising belligerent energies from that source.[37] Nothing could be more fascinating than the adventures of these letrados who, moved by motives ranging from candid idealism to frank opportunism, became secretaries of a revolutionary caudillo and attempted to prepare their rustic prince for the future establishment of a civilian government, while also waging a campaign of defamation against his adversaries. As they well knew, their real opponents in that campaign were the letrados of the other side, and their mud-slinging was always most enthusiastic when directed, not against the enemy caudillo, but against his secretaries.[38]

This was an experience reminiscent of the wars of independence, though we possess much less information about the letrados who served the caudillos of a hundred years earlier. The caudillo himself always held the limelight, and the secretary was merely "the stage manager, whose intervention is not perceived by the spectators, so absorbed in the main action."[39] Compared with the Mexican Revolution, there were more educated caudillos during the wars of independence, even if few could equal the exceptional intellectual gifts of Simón Bolívar. Still, alliances between illiterate caudillos and urban letrados did occur throughout the region at the time of independence, and the ambiguous relationship between them became an enduring pattern of Latin American political life in the nineteenth century. There was mutual admiration, but also lingering mistrust, between the brutal, personalist military commander and the doctor of laws — the manipulator of language, writing, and most importantly, political ideology — and the tension between the two often became extreme. In the Mexican Revolution, the practical disappearance of important social institutions — the army, the church, the academy — heightened the tensions inherent in encounters between headstrong individuals, representatives of worlds that seemed "irreconcilably" different and destined to collide. A first meeting between an urban letrado and the revolutionary caudillo Pancho Villa is thus described by novelist Martín Luis Guzmán:

At each question or answer from this side or that, one sensed a contact between two distinct worlds, irreconcilable in all ways, except for the coincidental alliance that allied them in this struggle. Poor deluded visionaries — for that's all we were at the time — we had gone to that place carrying only the flimsy experience provided by our books and our idealistic impulses. And what did we get? We got caught up, full force and by surprise, in the tragedy of good and evil, which cannot mix and where no compromise is possible, only victory or defeat. We were running from Victoriano Huerta — the traitor, the assassin — and we ended up, thanks to the generous dynamics of life itself, in the hands of Pancho Villa, whose soul, more than a man's soul, was the soul of a jaguar. He was a jaguar momentarily domesticated for the purposes of our work — or what we believed to be our work—a jaguar we petted, gliding our hands over his flanks and trembling lest he reach out suddenly with a swipe of his powerful claws.[40]

No caudillo lacked intellectual councilors who represented improvised revolutionary institutions, tried to reorganize the bureaucratic structures fractured by the conflict, and sometimes formed delegations to represent the revolution in diplomatic missions abroad. Not infrequently, they passed from one revolutionary entourage to another or were recruited among local representatives of the government, trading the pretentious pomp of some provincial town for a raggedly improvised headquarters in a military camp. Their acid testimony abounds, and it constitutes the only written record of the revolutionary ranks. Upon reading the most conspicuous authors of this group (Martín Luis Guzmán, José Vasconcelos, Mariano Azuela) one is struck by their personal, individual perspective, so distant from the sociological analysis applied by scholarly studies of the social processes unleashed by the revolution as a whole.[41]

It is suggestive that the early writings of letrados involved in the revolution grant such large importance to the role of intellectuals in the rebel camps, whether as the councilors and private secretaries of insurgent leaders or as the bureaucratic survivors of a previous regime, waiting patiently for the moment when their services will be required once more: "Being in the revolution is a sure way to get rich, and being in the government is the only way to stay rich and make one's fortune grow as it should. But just as a rifle is indispensable for the revolution, an office clerk is indispensable for the government."[42] Mariano Azuela specialized in critiques of intellectuals, members of a social group which he despised despite belonging to it himself. In his famous novel *Los de abajo,* Azuela placed the rude war captain Demetrio in the center of a triangle formed by three "doctoral" characters representing the plural participation of intellectuals in the revolution: Cervantes, Solís, and Valderrama. We have a good understanding of the progressive elaboration of *Los de abajo,* beginning with its first publication in an El Paso newspaper (1915), and can trace the sharpening caricature of the intellectual opportunist

(Cervantes), contrasted to the disillusioned idealist (Solís) that the author himself had become during his own participation in the forces of Pancho Villa.[43] The third character (Valderrama) portrays an intellectual who participates authentically in the revolutionary impulse, but who can endure its vicissitudes only by retreating into insanity. The "loco" Valderrama thus joins a long literary tradition of "madmen," enabled by their condition to see the truth and to endure its aberrations.

Azuela's paradigm of intellectuals in the revolution has a long tradition in Latin America and draws on a commonplace of the popular imagination regarding the representatives of the lettered city: an undisguised awe of the intellectual's capacity to manipulate language, whether in oratory or writing. In revolutions, it falls to the letrado to compose the documents that provide satisfying ideological justifications of the struggle, the requisite glorifications of revolutionary leaders, and the plans coordinating scattered forces. On the other hand, there is an abiding lack of confidence in the letrado's perseverance and true solidarity with those who stand outside the lettered city, a suspicion that the fruits of the revolution will be lost through the treachery of a letrado. After Azuela, others would explain this as a matter of class difference between the letrados and the other revolutionaries. But we could inscribe it as well in the traditionally problematic relationship between two forms of power, that which rests on the sword, and the other, which flows from the pen.

NOTES

I The Ordered City

1 See J. H. Parry, *The Cities of the Conquistadores* (London: Hispanic and Luso-Brazilian Councils, 1961); Rodolfo Quintero, *Antropología de las ciudades latinoamericanas* (Caracas: Dirección de Cultura de la Universidad Central de Venezuela, 1964); James R. Scobie, *Argentina: A City and a Nation* (New York: Oxford University Press, 1964); Jorge E. Hardoy, ed., *Urbanization in Latin America: Approaches and Issues* (Garden City: Anchor Books, 1975); Jorge E. Hardoy and Richard Schaedel, eds., *Las ciudades de América Latina y sus áreas de influencia a través de la historia* (Buenos Aires: SIAP, 1975); José Luis Romero, *Latinoamérica: las ciudades y las ideas* (Mexico City: Siglo XXI, 1976); Jorge E. Hardoy and Richard Schaedel, eds., *Asentamientos urbanos y organización socio-productiva en la historia de América Latina* (Buenos Aires: SIAP, 1977).

2 Robert Ricard, *La "conquête espirituelle" du Mexique* (Paris: Institut d'Ethnologie, 1933); Silvio Zavala, *La filosofía política de la conquista de América* (Mexico City: Fondo de Cultura Economica, 1947).

3 See Immanuel Wallerstein, *The Modern World-System,* 2 vols. (New York: Academic Press, 1974–80).

4 Jorge E. Hardoy, *El modelo clásico de la ciudad colonial hispanoamericana* (Buenos Aires: Instituto Tocuato di Tella, 1968).

5 George M. Foster, *Culture and Conquest: America's Spanish Heritage* (New York: Wenner-Gren Foundation for Anthropological Research, 1960).

6 Lewis Mumford pointed out that Hippodamus's "true innovation consisted in realizing that the form of the city was the form of its social order": *The City in History* (New York: Harcourt, Brace & World, 1961), 172.

7 Michel Foucault, *Les mots et les choses, une archéologie des sciences humaines* (Paris: Gallimard, 1966), 92–136.

8 Op. cit., in Spanish translation (Mexico City: Siglo XXI, 1968), 64–65.

9 *Colección de documentos inéditos relativos al descubrimiento, conquista, y colonización* (Madrid, 1864–1884), 34: 280, emphasis added.

10 Giulio Argan, *The Renaissance City* (New York: George Brazilier, 1969).

11   Foucault, *Les mots*, 78.

12   Marios Camhis, *Planning Theory and Philosophy* (London: Tavistock Publications, 1979).

13   Clifford Geertz, "Ideology as a Cultural System" in *Ideology and Discontent* ed. David E. Apter (New York: Free Press, 1964); Clifford Geertz, *The Interpretation of Cultures* (New York: Basic Books, 1973).

14   Antoine Arnauld and Pierre Nicole, *La logique ou l'art de penser,* ed. Pierre Clair and François Girbal (Paris: P.U.F., 1965), 53.

15   Ibid., 54.

16   Peter Gay, *The Enlightenment: An Interpretation. The Rise of Modern Paganism* (New York: The Norton Library, 1977), 36.

17   Pierre Chaunu, *L'Amérique et les Amériques* (Paris: Armand Colin, 1964), 12.

18   Nevertheless, see the work by a disciple of Frederick Jackson Turner, applying the thesis to Latin America: Alistair Hennessy, *The Frontier in Latin American History* (Albuquerque: University of New Mexico Press, 1978).

19   Richard Konetzke, *América Latina, II: La época colonial* (Madrid: Siglo XXI, 1972), 119.

20   On the adaptation of the Greek urban ethos to the new conditions of the New World, see Richard Morse, "A Framework for Latin American Urban History," in *Urbanization in Latin America,* ed. Hardoy.

21   Fernand Braudel, *Civilisation matérielle, économie et capitalisme, XVe–XVIIIe siecle,* vol. 3, *Le temps du monde* (Paris: Armand Colin, 1979), 343.

22   Thomas Gage, *Nueva relación que contiene los viajes de Thomas Gage en la Nueva España* (Guatemala City: Biblioteca Guatemala, 1946; first edition: London, 1648).

23   Braudel, *Civilisation matérielle,* 25.

24   Stanley and Barbara Stein, *The Colonial Heritage of Latin America* (New York: Oxford University Press, 1970).

25   Braudel, *Civilisation matérielle,* 338.

2   The City of Letters

1   Juan Sánchez Baquero, *Fundación de la Compañía de Jesús en la Nueva España* (Mexico City: Editorial Patria, 1945).

2   Quoted by Braudel, *Civilisation matérielle,* 368.

3   Joaquín García Icazbalceta, *Documentos franciscanos siglos XVI y XVII,* 2 vols., ed. Códice Mendieta (Mexico, n.p., 1902).

4   José Antonio Maravall, *La cultura del barroco* (Barcelona: Ariel, 1975).

5 Arnold Hauser, *The Social History of Art* vols. 8–10 (London: Routledge & Kegan Paul, 1951).

6 Pedro Ureña Henríquez, *Las corrientes literarias en la América Hispánica* (Mexico City: Fondo de Cultura Económica, 1949), 87.

7 Mariano Picón Salas, *De la conquista a la independencia,* 2nd ed. (Mexico City: Fondo de Cultura Económica, 1950), 101; and Alejo Carpentier, *Tientos y diferencias* (Mexico City: UNAM, 1964).

8 Karl Mannheim, *Essays on the Sociology of Culture* (London: Routledge [& Kegan Paul], 1956) and *Essays on the Sociology of Knowledge* (New York: Oxford University Press, 1952).

9 Alvin W. Gouldner, *The Dialectic of Ideology and Technology* (New York: Seabury Press, 1976) and *The Future of Intellectuals and the Rise of the New Class* (New York: Seabury Press, 1979).

10 Justo Sierra, *Mexico social y político* (1899), in *Evolución política del pueblo mexicano* (Caracas: Biblioteca Ayacucho, 1977), 308.

11 I have attempted a political and ideological reading of Fernán González de Eslava in my essay "La señal de Jonás sobre el pueblo mexicano," in *Escritura* 5, no. 10 (July–December 1980): 179–239.

12 Italian original: "l'occhio non vede cose ma figure di cose chi significano altre cose."

13 Italo Calvino, *Le citta invisibili* (Torino: Einaudi, 1972), 22.

3 The City of Protocols

1 Gilberto Freyre, *Ordem e progresso* (Rio de Janeiro: José Olympio, 1959), 1:200.

2 See V. A. Ferguson, "Diglossia" (1959) in *Language and Social Context,* ed. Pier Paolo Giglioli (London: Penguin Books, 1972); Joshua A. Fishman, "Bilingualism with and without Diglossia; Diglossia with and without Bilingualism," *Journal of Social Issues* 23 (1967); and Ralph W. Fasold, *The Sociolinguistics of Society,* vol. 1, (Oxford: Basil Blackwell, 1984).

3 *Relaciones históricas* (Mexico City: Biblioteca del Estudiante Universitário — UNNAM, 1972), 133.

4 I discuss this problem in "La señal de Jonás."

5 Eugenio Coseriu, "Sistema, norma, y habla," in *Teoría del lenguaje y lingüística general,* 3rd ed. (Madrid: Gredos, 1978).

6 Angel Rosenblat, *Los conquistadores y su lengua* (Caracas: Ediciones de la Biblioteca, 1977).

7 *Cartas de Indias* (Madrid: Imprenta de Manuel G. Hernández, 1977; fac-simile edition: Guadalajara, 1970), 2:468.

8 Angel Rosenblat, *Los conquistadores.*

9 *Relaciones históricas,* 132–33.

10 Alejo Carpentier, *Tientos y diferencias,* 2nd ed. (Montevideo: Arca, 1970), 35–37.

11 I have analyzed this point in my essay "La tecnificación narrativa," *Hispanoamérica* 10, no. 30 (1981): 38–40.

12 Bernal Díaz del Castillo, *Historia verdadera de la conquista de la Nueva España* (Mexico: Espasa Calpe, 1955), 430–31.

13 Emilio de Carilla, ed., *El lazarillo de ciegos caminantes* (Barcelona: Labor, 1973), 284. Carrió de la Vandera adds that the custom of carving names was already very old by the late eighteenth century, having become "so common in America that there is no shelter or cave unadorned by names and obscene words."

14 Javier Ocampo López, "El proceso político, militar, y social de la Independencia," in *Manual de la historia de Colombia* (Bogotá: Instituto Colombiano de la Cultura, 1978–79), 2:57.

15 José Luis Romero, ed., *Pensamiento político de la Emancipación* (Caracas: Biblioteca Ayacucho, 1977), 1:173.

16 Joaquín Fernández de Lizardi, *El periquillo sarniento,* ed. Jefferson Rea Spell (Mexico: Porrúa, 1949), 1:23.

17 Ibid., 1:28.

18 Ibid., 1:20.

19 Series of articles published in *El tiempo of Buenos Aires* in 1828, collected in Félix Weinberg, "Juan Cruz Varela, crítico de la literatura nacional," *Boletín de la literatura argentina* 1, no. 1 (1964): 29–63.

20 Simón Rodríguez, "Sociedades americanas en 1828," in *Obras completas* (Caracas: Universidad de Simón Rodríguez, 1975), 1:267.

21 Ibid., 1:283.

22 Ibid., 1:285 and 1:287.

23 Ibid., 1:273.

24 Ibid., 1:243.

25 Ibid., 1:242.

26 Ferdinand de Saussure, *Curso de lingüística general* (Buenos Aires: Losada, 1979), 73.

27 Rodríguez, *Obras completas,* 1:237.

4 The Modernized City

1 José Pedro Varela, *De la legislación escolar* (Montevideo: Imprenta "El Nacional," 1876), 81–82. Earlier in the same work (on page 64), Varela denounced the

false contrast established by liberalism between civilian and caudillo rule: "Our political organization . . . with its complicated mechanism, with its multiplicity of functions and plethora of functionaries, presupposes the existence of a population schooled in the practice of democratic institutions. As a result of this supposition, and of the contradictory reality, we live a lie and experience a permanent state of disappointment. Our laws say one thing, and the facts say another. The words are often beautiful while the accompanying acts are evil, and the lies of those in power are not less audacious or transparent than the lies of those out of power."

2 Varela, *De la legislación escolar,* 68. On page 85, Varela says further about the relationship between contending political forces: "There is usually . . . antagonism in their words, but in reality there exists a close union between the two sorts of error that they respectively represent: the error of ignorance and the error of presumptuous, superficial knowledge. The autocratic tendencies of the rural caudillo do not really stray far from the oligarchic tendencies of the urban class that believes itself so superior. Each assists the other. The spirit of the university lends a veneer of cultivation to the political influence emanating from the countryside, while rural power allows the university to retain its social privileges along with ostensible control of the government."

3 José María Samper, *Historia de un alma* (Bogotá: Biblioteca Popular de Cultura Colombiana, 1948), 2:171–72. Wrote Samper, in reference to his friendship with Torres Caicedo: "I had the idea that it was indeed possible to have a liberal conservatism, or a conservative liberalism, acceptable to all patriotic, sincere, and disinterested men in pursuit of good."

4 Richard M. Morse (with Michael L. Conniff and John Wibel), *The Urban Development of Latin America, 1750–1920* (Stanford: Center for Latin American Studies, 1971); and Nicolás Sánchez Albornoz, "Gobernar es poblar" in *La población de América Latina* (Madrid: Alianza Universal, 1977).

5 José Luis Romero, *Latinoamérica: las ciudades y las ideas* (Mexico City: Siglo XXI, 1976), 252.

6 Claudio Véliz, *The Centralist Tradition of Latin America* (Princeton: Princeton University Press, 1980), 234–35.

7 Darcy Ribeiro, *Las Américas y la civilización,* 2nd ed. (Buenos Aires: Centro Editor de América Latina, 1972), 468.

8 Justo Sierra, *Periodismo político,* vol. 4 of *Obras completas,* ed. Agustí Yáñez (Mexico City: UNAM, 1977). The following declaration of principles, taken from his 1878 political campaign in *La libertad,* echoes the previously cited Samper quotation about liberal-conservatism: "Consequently, we declare liberty incomprehensible without its orderly realization, and that makes us conservatives; nor can we comprehend an order that does not follow a normal impulse toward progress, and that makes us liberals."

Notes   131

9 Rui Barbosa, *Obras completas,* vol. 29 (Rio de Janeiro: Ministério de Educação e Saúde, 1953), part 2:92–93. Elsewhere he asked: "With what else, other than words, can laws be made? Life, property, honor — all that is most essential to us will always depend on a choice of words." Ibid., part 3:304.

10 See Oliveira Lima's essay "As linguas castelhana e portugesa na América" (1906) in *Impressões da América espanhola (1904–1906),* ed. Manoel da Silveira Cardoso (Rio de Janeiro: José Olympio, 1953).

11 This point is addressed in my prologue to Rubén Darío, *Poesía* (Caracas: Biblioteca Ayacucho, 1977) and in my essay "Indagación de la ideología en la poesía (Los dípticos seriados de *Versos sencillos*)" en *Revista iberoamericana* (July–December 1980), 112–13.

12 [No editor], *Poesía gauchesca* (Caracas: Biblioteca Ayacucho, 1977), 192.

13 See Antônio Cândido, *O método crítico de Sílvio Romero,* Boletim no. 266, 2nd ed. (São Paulo: FFCLUSP, 1963).

14 Jean Franco, "What's in a Name? Popular Culture Theories and their Limitations," in *Studies in Latin American Popular Culture* 1 (1982), 7.

15 E. Bradford Burns, "Cultures in Conflict: The Implications of Modernization in Nineteenth-Century Latin America," in *Elites, Masses, and Modernization in Latin America, 1850–1930* (Austin: University of Texas Press, 1979), 76–77.

16 The best Mexican example is Justo Sierra, *Evolución política del pueblo mexicano* (1900), to which José C. Valadés might well be referring (despite calling it an exception to his criticism of Porfirian historiography) in the following quotation: "It was during the Porfirian regime that official history became solidly entrenched. That history, child of an unnatural peace, was forged by the literary champions of the regime, and it covered with a heavy mantel of authority the ideas, the men, and the facts that seemed to contradict its pacifist encantations. The few real figures and ideas it retained in its pages were mere adornments." *El porfirismo. Historia de un regimen. El crecimiento* (Mexico City: Patria, 1979), xxv.

17 Leopoldo Lugones, *El payador* (Caracas: Biblioteca Ayacucho, 1979), 14.

18 Ibid., 15.

19 See François Bourricard, "Algunas características de la cultura mestiza en el Perú contemporáneo," *Revista del Museo Nacional* 23 (1954); also my essay "El área cultural andina (hispanismo, mesticismo, indigenismo)," in *Cuadernos americanos* 33 (1974).

20 In *Mi diario* by Mexican author Federico Gamboa, one reads a complaint dated 12 April 1894: "Since any day now a demolition crew will arrive and leave not a trace of it, there should be at least a sketch of this unappreciated pharmacy of Coliseo Street, a place that all Mexico City has known for years." And, in a later entry from 25 April 1895: "My Mexico City is disappearing! The old Iturbide Café, so full of character and local color, founded and owned ever since by the

French, has now passed into the hands of Yanquis, with brews from there and customers from there." José Emilio Pacheco, *Diario de Federico Gamboa* (Mexico City: Siglo XXI, 1977), 52–54.

21 See Carlos M. Rama, ed., *Utopismo socialista (1830–1893)* (Caracas: Biblioteca Ayacucho, 1977).

5 The Polis Politicized

1 Pedro Henríquez Ureña, *Las corrientes literarias en la América hispánica* (Mexico City: Fondo de Cultura, 1949), 165.

2 Even discounting the intellectuals whom Henríquez Ureña places earlier in "the period of organization" but whose political activities fall squarely between 1890 and 1920 (for example, Manuel González Prada), one name by itself is important enough to refute arguments concerning the supposedly apolitical nature of literatos in modernizing Latin America: José Martí (1853–1895). In 1890, Martí abandoned literary activity and journalism to devote himself to the Cuban struggle for independence. Another salient example is the refined Brazilian symbolist poet, João de Cruz e Souza (1861–1898), who never stopped writing about political matters. Cruz e Souza's political engagement is certainly understandable in a black man whose parents had once been slaves and who had to contend throughout his life with the marked racial prejudice of the day.

3 See Carlos Real de Azúa, *Historia visible e historia esotérica* (Montevideo: Calicanto-Arca, 1975).

4 From the article "Heredia," first published in *El economista americano* in New York (July 1888) and later collected in José Martí, *Nuestra América* (Caracas: Biblioteca Ayacucho, 1977), 205.

5 José Enrique Rodó, *Obras completas* (Madrid: Editorial Aguilar, 1967), 1374–45.

6 Carlos Real de Azúa, "El modernismo y las ideologías," *Escritura* 2 (Caracas, January–June 1977): 3.

7 Manuel González Prada, *Páginas libres, horas de lucha* (Caracas: Biblioteca Ayacucho, 1976), 96–97.

8 Jorge Ruedas de la Serna, from his prologue to Juan José Tablada, *Obras II: Sátira política* (Mexico City: UNAM, 1981), 9. Tablada's political function would have been more evident if this volume had also included the exalted praise of Venustiano Carranza (revolutionary foe of Díaz and Huerta) that Tablada felt obliged to provide later as a diplomatic representative of Mexico in Colombia and Venezuela.

9 (Caracas: Biblioteca Ayacucho, 1977).

10   The contents of this book were foreshadowed in articles published by Vallenilla Lanz in *El cojo ilustrado* between 1905 and 1913. See also his *Obras completas*,
vol. 1 (Caracas: Centro de Investigaciones Históricas, Universidad Santa María,
1983) and [no author], *Vallenilla, aristócrata del oprobio: Sentencia de la Comisión
Investigadora de enriquecimiento ilícito* (Caracas: Ediciones Centauro, 1971).

11   Reyes Spindola, a member of the Porfirian circle of "Científicos," elimi-
nated the authors' names from articles in *El Universal* from the time of the paper's
founding.

12   José Enrique Rodó, "Impresiones de un drama," in *El mirador de Próspero*
(1913), *Obras completas*, 539–45.

13   Francisco Bulnes discusses similar matters in *El Verdadero Díaz y la revolución* (Mexico City: Eusebio Gómez de la Puente, 1920). Rama provides the
author but not the exact source of the quotation [translator's note].

14   Cuban thinkers of the 1920s were later to criticize Martí's emphasis on a
multi-class alliance because of the resulting postponement of the legitimate demands of the poor.

15   Rufino Blanco Fombona, *La novela de dos años* corresponds to Fombona's
diaries for 1904–1905.

16   *Rufino Blanco Fombona íntimo* (Caracas: Monte Avila, 1975), 53.

17   John J. Johnson, *Political Change in Latin America* (Stanford: Stanford University Press, 1958) advanced a thesis later modified by H. Bernstein in the *Hispanic American Historical Review* 40 (1960). For a detailed evaluation, see Juan F.
Marsal, *Cambio social en América Latina* (Buenos Aires: Solar/Hachette, 1967).

18   The content of this book was prefigured four years earlier in a course
taught by Caso in the Escola de Altos Estudios.

19   Albert Hirschman, *The Passions and the Interests: Political Arguments for
Capitalism before its Triumph* (Princeton: Princeton University Press, 1977).

20   Luis Eduardo Nieto Arteta and Luis Ospina Vásquez, "The Turn to Authoritarianism in Latin America and the Search for its Economic Determinants,"
in *The New Authoritarianism in Latin America,* ed. David Collier (Princeton:
Princeton University Press, 1979), 63–64.

21   Karl Mannheim, *Ensayos de sociología de la cultura* (Madrid: Aguilar, 1957),
243–45.

6   The City Revolutionized

1   Abelardo Villegas, *Reformismo y revolución en el pensamiento latinoamericano*
(Mexico: Siglo XXI, 1972), 6.

2   Véliz, *The Centralist Tradition,* 281.

3 José Luis Romero, *La experiencia argentina y otros ensayos* (Buenos Aires: Editorial de Belgrano, 1980), 27.

4 Raúl Prebisch, "Capitalism: the second crisis," *Third World Quarterly* 3 (July 1981): 3.

5 Pedro Henríquez Ureña, *La utopía de América* (Caracas: Biblioteca Ayacucho, 1978), 367–73.

6 Pedro Henríquez Ureña remarked on the existence of this "intermediate generation" (to which he himself belonged) in a note in his book *La corrientes literarias en la América Hispánica,* 265, though he did no more than provide a list of authors who composed it.

7 The phrase was recorded by José Vasconcelos in his *Ulises criollo: Memorias* (Mexico City: Fondo de Cultura Económica, 1982), 1:333. In the same work, one can contrast an appreciation of rural folklore with a negative view of productions of contemporaneous popular culture such as the distressingly successful song "La cucaracha."

8 Alberto Zum Felde, *Indice crítico de la literatura hispanoamericana. El ensayo y la crítica* (Mexico City: Editorial Guarania, 1954), 214.

9 Manuel González Prada, *Páginas libres, horas de lucha* (Caracas: Biblioteca Ayacucho, 1976), 107, 201–202, and 214.

10 Cited in Bruno Podestá, *Pensamiento político de González Prada* (Lima: Instituto Nacional de Cultura, 1975), 31.

11 González Prada, *Páginas libres,* 210.

12 Letter to Ricardo J. Areco, 1910, in Rodó, *Obras completas,* 1065.

13 Letter to Luis A. Thevent, 1916, in Rodó, *Obras completas,* 1086.

14 Milton I. Vanger, *The Model Country: José Batlle y Ordóñez of Uruguay, 1907–1915* (Hanover, N.H.: University Press of New England, 1980). Anarchist organizations refused to take part in party politics. The same attitude impregnated the political vision of Manuel González Prada, and it also helps explain some of the problems that José Martí encountered in organizing the Partido Revolucionario Cubano, as recorded in certain passages of the articles that he published in *Patria.*

15 José Martí, *Obras completas* (Havana: Editorial Nacional, 1963), 1:178.

16 Ibid., 1:124.

17 See articles by Ibrahíam Hidalgo Paz, Diana Abad, and Juan Carlos Mirabal in *Anuario del Centro de Estudios Martianos* 4 (1981) and by Salvador Morales in *Anuario Martiano* 6 (1976).

18 Arturo Andrés Roig, *Los krausistas argentinos* (Pueblas: José M. Cajica, 1969) and Arturo Ardao, *Batlle y Ordóñez y el positivismo filosófico* (Montevideo: Número, 1951).

19 Nordau's comments were recorded by Enrique Gómez Carrillo, *Almas y cerebros* (Paris: Garnier, 1898), 248–49.

20 Abelardo Villegas, *Reformismo y revolución*, 192.

21 See Joyce Waddell Bailey, "The Penny Press," in *Posada's Mexico* ed. Ron Tyler (Washington: Library of Congress, 1979), 85–121.

22 James D. Cockcroft, *Precursores intelectuales de la Revolución mexicana* (Mexico City: Siglo XXI, 1971).

23 "They maintained their contact with the people. The smallness of the city permitted it, and that was a great advantage," wrote Octavio R. Amadeo, *Vidas argentinas* (Buenos Aires: Bernabé y Cía, 1940), 144.

24 José Luis Romero, *Latinoamérica: Las ciudades y las ideas* (Mexico City: Siglo XXI, 1971).

25 Martín García Merou, *Recuerdos literarios* (Buenos Aires: La Cultura Argentina, 1916), 266.

26 J. Galante de Sousa, *O teatro no Brasil* (Rio de Janeiro: Ed. de Ouro, 1968), 277.

27 Gerard Behágue, *Music in Latin America: An Introduction* (Englewood Cliffs, N.J.: Prentice Hall, 1979), 96–97.

28 According to R. Magalhães Júnior, *A vida vertiginosa de João do Rio* (Rio de Janeiro: Civilização Brasileira, 1978), 81, Lansac paid the author's royalties in advance of each printing. For the 1907 printing they amounted to 359,000 réis, 10 percent of the cover price.

29 Edgard Carone, *Movimento operário no Brasil (1877–1944)* (São Paulo: Difel, 1979), 42–47.

30 John M. Hart, *Los anarquistas mexicanos, 1860–1900* (Mexico City: SepSetentas, 1974) and *Anarquismo y clase obrera en México* trans. María Luisa Puga (Mexico City: Siglo XXI, 1980); Gastón García Cantú, *El socialismo en México, siglo XIX* (Mexico City: Ediciones Era, 1969); and Cockcroft, *Precursores intelectuales*.

31 Alberto Zum Felde, *Proceso intelectual del Uruguay* (Montevideo: Editorial Claridad, 1941), 214.

32 Horacio Quiroga, "La profesión literaria," in *El hogar* (1928), quoted from *Sobre literatura* (Montevideo: Arca, 1970), 90.

33 Manuel Gálvez, *Recuerdos de la vida literaria. I: Amigos y maestros de mi juventud* (Buenos Aires: Librería Hachette, 1961), 36.

34 See *Revista de la Biblioteca Nacional* 18 (1978): 9–39.

35 Horacio Quiroga, "La crisis del cuento nacional," *La Nación* (1928), quoted from *Sobre literatura*, 95.

36 Carlos Monsivais, "Notas sobre la cultura mexicana en el siglo XX," in *Historia general de Mexico* (Mexico City: El Colegio de México, 1976), 4:360.

37 See Héctor Aguilar Camín, "Los jefes sonorenses de la Revolución Mexicana," in *Saldos de la revolución: Cultura y política en México, 1910–1980* (Mexico City: Nueva Imagen, 1982).

38   On the ideas of this generation of revolutionary intellectuals, see Enrique
Krauze, *Caudillos culturales en la Revolución mexicana* (Mexico City: Siglo XXI,
1976).

39   José M. Ramos Mejía, *Las multitudes argentinas* 2nd ed. (Madrid: Victoriano Suárez Editor, 1912), 205. In his long reconstruction of the secretaries
(often called "escribanos") of the wars of independence, Ramos Mejía stresses
"the constant exhibition of ill-digested readings that formed their baggage" in
order to show the oratorical emphasis that one also finds among the secretaries of
caudillos in the Mexican Revolution. "Their verbal pyrotechnics were full of pretty
lights and phosphorescence; their music, of drums and brass (though appropri-
ately plaintive, with tragic tremolos when the unfailing ill fortunes of the *Patria*
appeared amid choriambic rhythms) as comical here as lively and energetic in
ancient tragedies. Having composed the pretentious communiqué, manifesto, or
proclamation, they read it aloud, and therein lay the key to its magnetic effect.
They declaimed with art and special intentions, lifting the voice, alternately irate
or suffering, according to the requirements of each paragraph, with a preacher's
gestures, wherever the simple reading of the document or the sound of a patriotic
air was not enough to produce the desired effect." Compare this with Martín Luis
Guzmán's stylistic analysis of a proclamation by Alvaro Obregón a hundred years
later: "The worst of the manifesto — or the best, from the point of view of hu-
mor — did not lie in the play of similes and metaphors. It could be felt in the opening words ("The hour has arrived . . . ") and in the thunderous closing apostro-
phe ("Damn you!") and found its perfect expression in the following phraseology
of acutely theatrical dynamism: "History retreats in horror upon seeing that it will
have to open its pages to that glut of monstrosity" — the monstrosity of Huerta.
(*El águila y la serpiente,* in ed. Antonio Castro Leal, *La novela de la Revolución
Mexicana* bk. I (Mexico City: Aguilar, 1960), 165–388.

40   Luis Guzmán, *El águila,* 1:231.

41   For example, see Jesús Silva Herzog, *El agrarismo mexicano y la reforma
agraria* (Mexico City: Fondo de Cultura Economica, 1964), Arnaldo Córdova,
La ideología de la revolución mexicana (Mexico City: Ediciones Era, 1982), and
James D. Cockcroft, *Mexico, Class Formation, Capital Accumulation, and the State*
(New York: Monthly Review Press, 1983).

42   Such is the conviction of one of the characters of *Las moscas* (in *La novela de
la Revolución Mexicana,* 172), a work in which Azuela criticizes both bureaucracy
and the backward intellectuals of modernism.

43   Stanley L. Robe, *Azuela and the Mexican Underdogs* (Berkeley: University
of California Press, 1979), esp. 103–13.

INDEX

Independence period, 40–49
Ingenieros, José, 78

Korn, Alejandro, 78
Krausism in Latin America, 110–11

Landívar, Rafael, 42
Letrados: autodidacts among, 118–
19; and caudillos, 41, 122–25, 137;
differentiation among, 52–53, 75–
76; as functionaries, 18–24, 33–35;
as ideologues, 78–80, 84, 94–96,
107–108; as journalists, 52, 88–89;
as manipulators of legal protocols,
30–31; and the middle class, 94; as
philosophers, 86–87; as poets, 18;
political role of, 22–23, 76–80, 83–
87, 91–94; in Porfirian Mexico,
86–93; and the problem of patronage, 43, 89–90, 116–17; as
propagandists, 20, 85–86, 91–92;
as revolutionaries, 105, 109, 122–
25; social ascendancy of, 23–24,
46
Linguistic variants: influence of peninsular norms, 33, 37; and National Academies, 59–60; preva-
lence of diglossia, 31–32, 35–37;
vernacular American speech, 32
Literature: appropriations of "Nature" in, 60–61; European models
for, 116; markets for, 88–90, 116–
17, 120–21; in the construction of
national identities, 65–66
Lizardi, Joaquín Fernández de, 42–
43, 75
López, Lucio V., 71
López Velarde, Ramón, 121
Lugones, Leopoldo, 67, 77

Martí, José, 51, 61, 80–82, 89, 106,
109, 133 n.2
Mass-based party politics, 104–106
Mexican Revolution, 105, 122–25
Mistral, Gabriela, 102
Modernization: costumbrismo and,
64, 70–72; influence of Positivism
on, 56; internationalism and, 80–
82; and new legal codes, 58–59;
philologists in the service of, 58–
60; repressive features of, 68–69

Nariño, Antonio, 40–41
Nebrija, Elio Antonio de, 35, 44
Neruda, Pablo, 121

Oral tradition, appropriations of, 62–
65

Palma, Ricardo, 20, 71
Payró, Roberto, 117
Pérez Bonalde, Antonio, 61
Pérez Rosales, Vicente, 71
Pimentel, Francisco, 65
Podestá, Juan José, 111, 115
Popular Culture: musical manifesta-
tions of, 115–16; as a source of na-
tional identity, 66–68; new
twentieth-century prominence of,
103–104; theatrical manifestations
of, 114–15; urban myths of, 54–55
Posada, José Guadalupe, 50, 111

Quiroga, Horacio, 120–21

Rio, João do, 117, 136 n.28
Riva Palacio, Vicente, 71
Rivera, José Eustasio, 102
Reyles, Carlos, 94

Rodó, José Enrique, 78–79, 81–83, 89, 108

Rodríguez, Simón, 43–49, 59, 75, 103

Rojas, Ricardo, 65, 103

Romero, Sílvio, 64–65

Sabat Ercasty, Carlos, 121

Samper, José María, 51, 78

Sánchez, Florencio, 53, 95, 115

Sánchez Baquero, Juan, 16–17

Sanín Cano, Baldomiro, 78, 83, 121

Sarmiento, Domingo Faustino, 12, 43, 57, 77

Sierra, Justo, 15, 22, 57, 86

Sigüenza y Góngora, Carlos, 18, 23, 32

Silva, José Asunción, 84

Tablada, José Juan, 77, 86, 92

Torres, Carlos Arturo, 78, 81

Urban design: Baroque culture and, 2, 10; street nomenclature and, 25–27; symbolic systems and rationalization of, 3–9, 25–28; tension between ideal and real, 8–9, 27–28, 30, 73; utopian aspects of, 6–13

Urban growth and transformations, 51, 69–70, 113

Valencia, Guillermo, 77

Vallenilla Lanz, Laureano, 86, 96

Varela, José Pedro, 51, 57

Vargas, Vila, José Maria, 116

Vasconcelos, José, 57, 78, 100, 102, 105, 124

Vaz Ferreira, Carlos, 47, 49, 78

Wast, Hugo, 116

Zum Felde, Alberto, 105, 119

Angel Rama, one of Latin America's most distinguished twentieth-
century men of letters, was a noted literary critic, journalist, editor, publisher,
and educator. He left his native Uruguay following the military takeover
and taught at the University of Venezuela and the University of Maryland.
He died in 1983 in a plane crash near Madrid. John Charles Chasteen is
Professor of History at the University of North Carolina, Chapel Hill.
He is the translator and editor of Tulio Halperín Donghi's
The Contemporary History of Latin America, also
published by Duke University Press.

Library of Congress Cataloging-in-Publication Data

Rama, Angel.
[Ciudad letrada. English]
The lettered city / Angel Rama ; edited and translated
by John Charles Chasteen.
p. cm. — (Post-contemporary interventions)
Includes index.
ISBN 0-8223-1757-5 (cloth:alk. paper). — ISBN 0-8223-1766-4
(pbk.:alk. paper)
1. Latin America — Intellectual life. 2. Cities and towns — Latin
America.
I. Chasteen, John Charles, 1955- . II. Title. III. Series.
F1408.3.R3213 1996
980 — dc20   96-13996
CIP